# Mountain Girl

# *Mountain Girl*

Rose Creasy McMills

REDEMPTION
PRESS

Published by Redemption Press, PO Box 427, Enumclaw, WA 98022.

Cover Illustration by Shirley M. Levesque.

©2013 Cover and Web design by Jonathan McMills
www.mountaingirlbook.com

ISBN 13: 978-1-63232-433-7 (Print)
        978-1-63232-434-4 (ePub)
        978-1-63232-435-1 (Mobi)
Library of Congress Catalog Card Number: 2009909283

*To Uncle Roy*

# Contents

# Chapter 1

## *Morning on the Farm*

UNCLE JOHN WOKE with a start to the sound of bouncing on the bed in the room above him. The old farmhouse had been silent and dark since his niece Elizabeth and her family had moved from the West Virginia homestead to New Mexico two years ago.

And now they were back. And his heart swelled in his chest and the corners of his lips twitched upward, trying for a smile at the giggles coming from overhead. He schooled his mouth back into its usual grimace. He was glad they were back; he must be careful not to let it show. He began carefully counting the cracks between the floorboards overhead like he did every morning.

Elizabeth had awakened before dawn, peering into the dampness of the upstairs bedroom over the edge of the quilts piled so high she could barely turn over. It was cool in the mountains, even in the summer.

It was raining outside the open window, drops splattering on the ledge. Rain outside pelted the tar paper roof, poured down into the gutters, and gushed into the rain barrel below. After two years in the desert, Elizabeth thought it was the most beautiful sound she had ever heard. She closed her eyes in bliss and fell back asleep.

The next time she woke up, it was morning and the rain had stopped. The sun was up and busy drying everything, and a breeze ruffled the white muslin curtains.

She fought with the blankets and sat upright in the bed, looking down at Annie, four, curled in a warm ball, hair mussed against the feather-tick mattress.

The room was the same. Blue-flowered paper covered the walls and the slanted ceiling. Here and there the roof had leaked, and stains in different shapes formed themselves into monsters in her active imagination.

A wasp was making loops across the ceiling. Elizabeth just knew the minute she tried to get out of bed, it would dive down and sting her. Suddenly it swooped and landed on the window pane, throwing itself furiously against the glass, then ducked under and flew out the opening.

*Moooooooooooo.*

Elizabeth knelt on the bed, pushed the curtains aside, and looked out. Five unhappy cows were outside the fenced-in yard. They wanted their breakfast, needed to be milked, and were calling for Grandpa to come out.

Petunia was the loudest. She had a *moo* that started low and ended high, like a boy whose voice was changing.

"It's true . . . I'm back," Elizabeth whispered to herself, afraid the farm would disappear if she spoke aloud.

"Annie," she shook her sister. "Annie, we're back!"

Annie turned over and burrowed into the covers like a chipmunk in its hole. Elizabeth stood up, her nightgown ballooning out, and jumped up and down on the bed. She felt younger than her eleven years. The two hard years living in New Mexico while Daddy taught at the college there melted away. She bounced and sang, "Lazy old Annie, will you get up, will you get up, will you get up? Lazy old Annie, will you get up, will you get up todayyyyyy?"

Soon Annie was awake and bouncing too—the two girls holding hands and shrieking.

Then Elizabeth hopped down and pulled on the dress she had worn the day before—the last day of their trip back. She looked at her cowboy boots sitting beside the bed and wrinkled her nose slightly. She could still see the desert dust powdering them.

"Barefoot for me!" she said saucily to Annie, putting her fists on her hips.

Annie was unimpressed and had other priorities, sliding down the mound of quilts and going in search of Mama, sleeping downstairs with Sarah, one-and-a-half years old.

Elizabeth plunged down the stairs, crossed the living room in a couple of long-legged strides, and then stopped short to peek around into the kitchen. Two fry pans, one with bacon and one with eggs, sizzled and popped on the big black Acorn cookstove.

Grandma was standing at the counter making biscuits like she did first thing every morning. Her gnarled hands, crippled with arthritis, were covered with flour, and she was wielding the rolling pin like an orchestra conductor. She cut the raw biscuit dough in front of her, soft as any down pillow, into rounds and transferred them to a flat metal pan.

She was wearing a faded print dress and a bib apron of flour-sack cloth. Her long gray hair was in a bun at the back of her neck, and she had on heavy tan stockings and sturdy black shoes with thick heels. Her hair looked whiter and she seemed shorter than when Elizabeth had left.

Elizabeth romped into the kitchen and threw her arms around her, glorying that she was still warm and soft and smelled like apple butter.

"Land sakes, you like to scared me to death," Grandma gasped.

"I'm back! I'm back!" Elizabeth chanted in delight.

Grandma wiped her hands on a nearby dish towel and then wrapped her arms around Elizabeth. "Lookit how tall you growed," she said, kissing Elizabeth's forehead and smoothing back the long brown hair. Her eyes shimmered with tears.

Elizabeth pretended not to notice. "Where's Grandpa?" she asked, releasing herself.

"He's down milkin' cows with your daddy. Tell them to come up for breakfast now, you hear?" she called as Elizabeth barreled out of the kitchen.

In the living room, Elizabeth stopped short. Uncle John was sitting on a high-backed chair before the fireplace. He had tipped the chair forward on two legs and was warming his hands. He didn't look up and he didn't speak. His face might have been carved from stone.

Elizabeth knew the unwritten family rule that no one spoke to Uncle John and Uncle John spoke to no one, but her joy made her reckless.

"I'm back," she whispered and then watched in satisfaction when a muscle in Uncle John's jaw twitched.

"I'm back!" she shouted to the early-morning world as she burst out into the sunshine.

Down the hill across the little creek, she could see Grandpa and Daddy, sitting on little three-legged stools, milking cows tied to the split rail fence. Daddy had Petunia, a Guernsey, and Grandpa had White Face, who was red with a white face. The other cows were milling around, munching on a pile of hay and waiting their turn.

Each squirt of milk went *zingggg* into the zinc buckets.

Whichone, the cat, circled around hungrily, tail twitching. Grandpa aimed a stream of milk off to the side, and she scampered to it, lapping daintily at the creamy white puddle on the ground.

Then Elizabeth saw the mountains. They rose majestic blue in the morning mist, sheltering the farm like overweight guardian angels. She took a deep breath of the fragrant country air.

"Grandpa! Grandpa!" she called, running barefoot through the damp grass, slipping and falling, and getting up again. Then, buoyed by her own enthusiasm, she surprised herself by leaping the creek.

Daddy stood up when she fell, and Grandpa stood up when she jumped the creek. It was a different Elizabeth Grandpa saw than the one who had left for New Mexico—this Elizabeth was tall and slim with long brown legs, like a colt in springtime. He leaned on the cow's back, taking off his soft felt hat to swat the flies, and grinned at her. "Elizabeth Rose," he said. "All growed up."

Elizabeth came around the front of White Face, watching out for the cow's slobbery nose, and hugged Grandpa's tall, bony frame. He was wearing suspenders like always. "Grandma says breakfast is ready," she said, smiling up at him.

At breakfast that morning, Elizabeth thought her heart would just burst from happiness. Grandma and Grandpa sat at opposite ends of the long table. Grandpa was busy shoveling food in his mouth, wiping his white handlebar moustache in between bites. Grandma was busy directing traffic.

"Willie," she said to Daddy, "you send those biscuits round again. Elizabeth Rose, you eat up now—we got to put some flesh on you. Katherine, that baby needs some more oats." Grandma extended a serving spoon dripping with oatmeal in Sarah's direction.

"She's fine, Rose. Thanks, anyway," Mama said, jogging Sarah on her lap. Mama's soft brown curls were caught back in a ribbon, and her skin glowed. Elizabeth thought she looked younger and caught Daddy looking at her.

Annie was tired from the trip and stared sullenly at her plate of biscuits and gravy, bacon, and fried eggs. Grandpa watched her from under his bushy white eyebrows and then leaned over and tickled her in the side. Annie glared at him, outraged, but when he patted his knee, she hopped down and crawled up in his lap.

Only Uncle John seemed unaware of the partylike atmosphere. He sat solidly in his chair, kept his eyes on his plate, and finished his breakfast in short order.

Once Elizabeth saw his eyes flicker around the table and rest on her for a second. It was a movement so quick that only she caught it.

Elizabeth had been thinking about Uncle John for two years. Wandering in the desert that surrounded their New Mexico home, with only horned toads for company, she had had a lot of time to think. Sometimes she had imaginary conversations with Uncle John.

"Why don't you ever talk to anyone?" she'd ask.

Uncle John's bright blue eyes would meet hers. "When I was a baby," he would begin, "a wicked witch, angered because Grandpa had cut down her favorite tree, put a curse on me. I would be able to speak to no one."

"And why doesn't anyone speak to you?"

"That was part of the curse. I can hear no one except the beautiful young girl who will break the spell."

"How will the girl break the spell?"

Uncle John's sad eyes would gaze into the mountains in the distance. "That's the part no one knows," he would say. And then he would fall silent again.

Elizabeth wondered who they could get to break the spell. She knew it couldn't be her because she was just a scrawny kid with freckles and a scraped knee. She looked for the girl in New Mexico but then decided she must be back in West Virginia. The only one Elizabeth could think of was Luisa Ann Moore, who lived in Craigsville. Luisa had long blond hair and big brown eyes. What Elizabeth didn't know was if Luisa was good. She was almost sure the beautiful young girl had to be good too.

# Chapter 2

## *Uncle John*

THE STORY ABOUT Grandpa cutting down the witch's tree and the curse was a lovely fantasy.

But now Elizabeth was eleven (although she still liked dolls) and didn't really believe in curses or witches (except sometimes), and the big question that preoccupied her was this: What was wrong with Uncle John?

There had to be something wrong with him because people hardly spoke to him and treated him like he wasn't really part of the family, although he had always lived in the big old farmhouse on its fifty acres along with everybody else.

In New Mexico, Elizabeth would lie in bed at night in the top bunk of their adobe house and look at the beams close enough above her head to reach up and touch and think about the West Virginia farm they had left behind. Memories would come to her like a slideshow in her head: Grandma working the old treadle sewing machine, her feet rocking back and forth rhythmically as the silver needle darted in and out. Grandpa pounding red-hot horseshoes into the right shape on an anvil, *clang, clang!* Aunt Lorena in one of her flour-sack print dresses, riding a horse bareback and barefoot and laughing when she got scolded. Her mom and dad sitting together on the back porch swing—the Rhododendron bush sweet smelling behind them.

Sometimes in the dark she'd count on her fingers all of Daddy's brothers and sisters: Dan, Jim, Joe, Charlie, Sarah, Luella, Myrtle, and Lorena. All of them grown now and gone from the farm. All teachers except for Uncle Joe, who was in the army, and Aunt Lorena, the youngest, away at business school in Charleston but home during the summer.

And then there was Uncle John, who had never left home and was a silent presence in the old farmhouse. Why was that? When Elizabeth was small, she had just taken it for granted, but the older she got, the more it became a burning question in her mind.

Uncle John looked like the other McCrearys—that black Irish look, Grandpa called it, with dark, curly hair and light eyes—but he was smaller than the other men, with long, tapered fingers. While the rest of the family's gaze was open and frank, he looked away quickly if you met his eyes.

# Uncle John

He kept to himself, spending a lot of time in his small bedroom with its two doors—one that opened into the dining room and one that opened out onto the back porch. He often came and went by his back entrance so no one knew if he was in the house or not. He didn't participate in the work of the farm. Every day he ate breakfast in the kitchen and then trudged the three miles over the mountain to Boone's Dairy, where he was hired to help with the morning milking.

On Sundays he walked to Calvin Bible Church. Elizabeth wondered why he didn't go to Alderson Baptist Church with the rest of the family. Sometimes he went to Bud's Grocery in Calvin. Elizabeth would see him walking down the dirt road that led out of the farm and returning hours later clutching a brown paper bag—a poke, Grandma called it. Several times he brought back horehound candy for Elizabeth and Annie, handing it to them without comment. No one ever offered him one of the horses or Patrick the Mule to ride on those long treks, and he never asked.

The only time he was together with the family was at meals. His chair was the one down at the far end of the table—the starvation end, Grandpa said—near the door to his room. He'd come out, eat, and go back in without saying a word. No one spoke to him except maybe Grandma when she said, "More taters, John?" and he silently took the dish.

Elizabeth was nine when Daddy got a teaching job in New Mexico, and she hadn't realized how many questions she had about Uncle John. It seemed like they were barely out of the hills when they started popping up in her head.

Elizabeth had asked Daddy about him once. "Daddy, what's wrong with Uncle John?"

Daddy had paused uncomfortably. He had a bucket of lye soap and water and was scrubbing the horse's harnesses in the barn. "I don't know, Lizzie. He's always seemed different—fragile. Even as a little boy, whenever we had company, he'd go hide under the back porch. He doesn't fit in with some of the rough mountain men here. If he'd been born in a different time and place, things might have been different for him . . ." Daddy trailed off.

"Mama," Elizabeth whispered once at bedtime, "what's wrong with Uncle John?"

"Nothing, Lizzie." Mama kissed her shining hair. "He just forgot to grow up."

"Grandma, what's wrong with Uncle John?" she had asked softly as they were stringing green beans for supper one day when she was younger. Grandma carefully broke one end off a bean pulling the string down one side, then turned it over and did the same thing with the other side.

"Nothin's wrong with John," she said crisply.

But Aunt Lorena had always been eager to talk. Wearing pants (something Grandpa disapproved of) and sitting cross-legged on her bed upstairs, she prattled on.

"I'm the youngest and John's a lot older," she confided, brushing out her glossy, dark hair. "I always remember him off to hisself. We wasn't suppose to talk to him because he'd get upset." Aunt Lorena told Elizabeth the story of Uncle John going crazy in the fifth-grade classroom, yelling and knocking over desks, the students huddled in one corner, the little hunchback lady teacher determined to whip him for daydreaming.

Elizabeth wondered if the teacher was secretly a witch.

"He was real bright," Aunt Lorena had continued. "I was embarrassed by him, though, cause he was kind of, well . . . strange. But all my girlfriends were sweet on him—they said he was so handsome and mysterious. But then the boys would tease him and he'd fly into such a rage that Grandma finally just kept him home."

Mama was the only one who had always broken the unwritten family rule. Sometimes she spoke to John, even if he didn't speak back. Some Sundays she read the Bible aloud to him. And every winter, John went out and gathered black walnuts from the ground, peeled off their green outer shell, picked the sweet nuts out, and placed them in a pretty box to give to Mama for Christmas.

As far as Elizabeth could see, Uncle John was just different—but in a good way.

He was just so smart, for one thing. The Millers, neighbors from over the mountain, went to Calvin Bible Church and said Uncle John stood up and recited entire chapters of the Bible from memory without missing a word.

And Elizabeth knew that, like her, Uncle John loved to read. Several times late at night when she tiptoed back downstairs for a drink of water, she caught Uncle John sitting by the fire, a book tipped to catch the light of the embers. There was always a stack of books outside his door, and several times Elizabeth sneaked one, examined it, then put it back, hoping he wouldn't notice.

For another thing, he loved music. Elizabeth was forbidden to go into his room, but often she would hear him playing the fiddle and sneak over and sit on the floor outside his door to listen. He played tunes he heard on the radio, songs from church, records they played on the wind-up gramophone. Sometimes he made things up.

Uncle Dan and Daddy "picked" the banjo, Grandma played the organ at church while Mama sang, and Elizabeth took piano for a year when they lived in New Mexico, but Uncle John's fiddling was the most beautiful thing she'd ever heard.

Once he unexpectedly burst out of his door and discovered Elizabeth sitting against the wall. She scrambled to her feet, and they both just stood there, Uncle John's eyes darting back and forth. Then he went back in his room and closed the door, and the fiddling resumed.

# Uncle John

Elizabeth knew he liked to draw, too, because she'd found scraps of paper with pictures of the animals on them, and one Christmas he drew Grandma a big picture of her favorite snowball bush in bloom. Grandma hung it over the daybed in the corner of the living room.

Elizabeth knew he cared most of all for the farm animals—and they loved him. It was just people he couldn't get along with. He often went to the barn at dusk with a lantern to check on the horses bedded down for the night. Sometimes you'd see him sitting against the fence with Beezer, the hound dog, stroking his ears and talking to him, and twice Elizabeth saw him sneak Whichone into his bedroom.

Grandma had a picture of John as a young man, sitting on a stump, feeding a flock of ducks. Elizabeth loved to look at that picture because Uncle John looked so happy—almost smiling.

Surely the family didn't shun Uncle John just because he was different from the rest of them—all outgoing hard workers. The boys were big and strong, and even the girls could handle the horses and chop the head off the Sunday chicken if they had to.

Maybe it was something Uncle John had done in the past, Elizabeth thought—something terrible that turned everyone against him. But what could that have been, and why did no one ever talk about it? And what was to keep her from making the same mistake?

The trouble was that Uncle John liked everything Elizabeth did. If everyone could stop loving John, maybe they could stop loving Elizabeth.

And there was this about Uncle John that everybody was aware of, although no one spoke of it. He *knew* things. He knew when there was going to be a blizzard and when the cow was going to calve. Maybe that was it—maybe he was just *so* different that he made people nervous. Elizabeth must try not to be too different.

But most of all, the whole thing with Uncle John made her both sad and mad. It just didn't seem fair.

# Chapter 3

## *Kittens Comin'*

ONE DAY IT was pouring rain and nobody could work outside. Uncle John sat at the far end of the table, finishing Grandma's buttermilk pancakes. Elizabeth knew he couldn't go to work because the bridge over the Gauley River was flooded out. She chewed on a piece of bacon and watched him stealthily from under her eyelashes until he went out into the rain.

Suddenly she remembered what she'd been thinking about before she went to sleep the previous night.

"Grandma, where's Whichone?"

"I don't know where that cat's got to," Grandma said absently, reading the Bible while she ate breakfast and underlining with a little stub of pencil.

Whichone had a funny name. When Grandma needed a mouser for the granary, she went over to look at the Millers' batch of kittens. She pointed at the black-and-white one and said, "I'll take that one." The Millers said, "Which one?" all together, and Grandma laughed. She decided then and there to call the kitten Whichone. Grandma cackled and told the story any time someone asked her about the cat's name.

Whichone had a batch of kittens every fall and another in the spring. Mama said Whichone was due to have her kittens any time, so Elizabeth kept a close watch. After breakfast she put on her sweater and went out on the back porch. Rain was streaming off the roof into the downspout and pounding into the rain barrel at the corner of the house.

She could hardly see the hills in the distance because of the fog. In the backyard the apple tree's branches drooped with moisture, almost touching the ground.

"Whichone!" Elizabeth called. "Here, kitty, kitty, kitty."

No cat. She looked in the box lined with a burlap sack under the bench on the back porch. Then she squatted down at the edge of the rough boards to peer underneath the porch at the black, wet earth, getting her back pelted in the process. No cat's eyes glowing in the darkness there.

She went inside to the coat tree, got an umbrella, and stepped into her cowboy boots. Mama was washing dishes in a metal tub sitting on the kitchen stove. Annie was standing on a chair and wearing a big apron that touched her toes. She was drying importantly, the steam and the moisture in the air making her golden-brown hair—the color of Mama's—into ringlets.

"Mama, Lizzie's going out in the rain," she tattled.

Elizabeth shut the door and didn't hear Mama's reply. She sloshed over to the smokehouse. Big slabs of meat were hanging inside.

No Whichone.

She thought of the cellar under the smokehouse, but it was always cold and damp even on a sunny day and housed spiders and toads. Surely Whichone wouldn't go there to have her kittens.

She thought hard. The chicken house? No—filled with roosting chickens today. The granary? "The barn!" Elizabeth said aloud, triumphantly. She set out on the five-minute walk to the top of the next hill. Even with the umbrella and her boots, she got wet, tall weeds slapping against her bare legs and dampening her dress.

She saw the barn rise up in the mist as she came over the top of the hill. On the side facing the hard road was painted, "Chew Mail Pouch Tobacco. Treat Yourself to the Best."

The barn was warm and dark. Fanny and Maud, the workhorses, were dozing in their stalls, each with a back hoof cocked in the resting position.

"Here, kitty kitty." She heard something stir in the hayloft above. Carefully she climbed the wooden ladder and peered over the edge of the loft floor—hay piled in all directions. Over in the far corner she saw something white. Whichone!

But she hadn't had her kittens. She was lying very still and gave a little weak *mew* as Elizabeth came toward her. Elizabeth dropped to her knees and felt the cat's heaving side.

"What's the matter, kitty? Are you all right?"

Whichone was not all right. She twisted her soft body in the hay. Her little pink nose was bright red. She strained and pushed but no kittens came out.

Elizabeth felt afraid. What if Whichone died? Maybe she should pray.

Suddenly someone sneezed in the loft. Elizabeth jumped and stared as a mound of hay moved. Then Uncle John emerged, hay sticking to his hair and clothes. He was soaking wet with dark hair plastered to his forehead.

Neither one of them said a word. Uncle John knelt beside the cat and began to feel along her sides, whispering to himself. Whichone didn't protest but lay her head down in the hay and purred softly. Elizabeth watched, mesmerized, as Uncle John stroked the cat's body slowly and methodically from head to tail. He began to hum a tune Elizabeth had never heard before.

Whichone lay very still, and then suddenly her side knotted up and she raised her head and a kitten began to come out. Uncle John never stopped stroking or humming.

The first kitten was in a little silky bag. Out popped a second and then a third. Whichone was purring loudly. She delicately chewed the sack off each one and then washed all three briskly and nudged them close to her belly to nurse.

As they began to dry, Elizabeth could see there were two striped tabbies and one that was black-and-white like Whichone. "Oh, how cute!" She picked up a tabby and held it close, kissing its soft head. When she looked up, hay at the mouth of the trap door was waving slowly.

Uncle John was gone.

She put the kitten back down and Whichone promptly washed it all over again.

That night at supper, all Elizabeth could talk about was the kittens. Annie's eyes were big and her mouth was open in rapt attention, but no one else seemed to care—the birth and death of animals was part of the cycle of the farm.

"Didya hear, John?" Grandma said, raising her voice like he was deaf. "Whichone done had her kittens."

Uncle John continued to eat, and although Elizabeth watched him out of the corner of her eyes a long time, he never looked up.

# Chapter 4

## *Snowball*

T HE MILLERS DON'T know what to do with Snowball," Daddy said at supper one night.

Elizabeth stopped chewing, her mouth full of cornbread. The Millers lived on the next farm over and Snowball was their Shetland pony. Elizabeth had wanted a pony forever.

"What's the matter with him?" said Grandpa, reaching for more chicken.

"He's gone lame and with their kids gone, they can't afford to keep him." Daddy was watching Elizabeth. She began chewing again, but very fast.

"Costs a lot to winter that pony," Grandpa said. "Might have to be put down."

It seemed the conversation was going to end there. Elizabeth sat and looked at her plate—at the drumstick and mashed potatoes and gravy, green beans and cornbread. She couldn't eat another bite because of the lump in her throat.

She looked at Grandma, who was passing round the apple butter and didn't seem to be paying attention.

Several times she had been to the Millers' place to ride Snowball. He had a shaggy mane that got in his eyes. He was black-and-white—one side of his face was black with a brown eye, and one side was white with a blue eye. He limped, but only a little—like Grandma with her arthritis. What would happen to Snowball?

Then help came from an unexpected source. "Perfectly good pony!" Uncle John spat out with feeling. Everyone stopped eating and looked up. Uncle John never said anything at supper.

"We have lots of room here," Mama said, wiping Sarah's mouth. Sarah was sitting on one of the high-backed chairs on top of a Sears catalog and a pillow. A cloth diaper was tied around her waist and to the rungs of the chair.

"But who would take care of him?" Daddy asked.

"Who would ride him?" Grandpa added, and they all smiled at Elizabeth. She realized it was a conspiracy. She jumped up, knocking over her glass of milk. "I'll take care of him!"

Mama and Grandma grabbed napkins and began sopping up the milk, laughing and scolding, and Annie was sent to the kitchen to fetch the dishrag.

"Lizzie spilled it," she complained.

Elizabeth just sat in the middle of the mess and smiled.

The next day Elizabeth and Daddy went to get Snowball. They walked through the fields and over the mountains so Elizabeth could ride the pony back. Elizabeth wore her cowboy boots.

The meadows were bright with wildflowers and dozens of small white butterflies danced with each other, one resting delicately on Elizabeth's shoulder.

Daddy knew the names of all the plants and insects. Elizabeth didn't like bees, but he said bees were good. He had two honeybee hives in little houses he had built up against the bank. Sometimes Elizabeth saw him out there wearing a big hat with veils hanging down to protect him from stings. At supper they always had a dish of honey with fresh biscuits.

After the warm sun of the meadow, it was cool and shady under the trees of Tyler's Mountain. Spring Beauty blossoms turned the forest floor pink.

"We can have lunch at that big flat rock up ahead," Daddy said.

They ate hard-boiled eggs with bread and one of Grandma's buttermilk cookies the size of Elizabeth's hand. Afterwards they lay on their backs chewing on teaberry leaves and looking up at the blue sky through the canopy of trees fifty feet above.

Coming down the other side of the mountain, they could see the Millers' place. It looked like a toy farm in the distance with a tiny black-and-white pony tied outside the barn.

Elizabeth was so excited she ran the rest of the way. While Mr. Miller and Daddy talked, Elizabeth danced around Snowball. She whispered in his soft, hairy ears that she loved him and she promised to *always* bring him carrots. Snowball snuffled at her sleeve with his soft pink-and-black muzzle.

"You take care of that pony now, ya hear?" Mr. Miller called after them.

Elizabeth wished it took longer to get home. She sat proudly on the brown leather saddle that came with Snowball and sang all the way home. She sang "Whistle While You Work" from *Snow White,* which she had seen at the drive-in. She sang "Mockingbird Hill" from the radio and hummed "Foggy Mountain Breakdown" that Uncle Dan played on his banjo. She sang "Jesus Loves the Little Children" from church.

When they got home, it was late, and by the time they got Snowball bedded down in his stall, supper was over. Grandma was waiting.

"Sakes alive, it's almost bedtime!" she said. She had saved them both big bowls of navy bean soup with salt pork, homemade applesauce, and a big plate of tomatoes.

Elizabeth was hungry but so tired she could hardly eat.

"Please, Mama, can I sleep in the barn tonight?" she begged, using her whiney voice.

"No, you may not," Mama said with a laugh.

Mama sat on the edge of Elizabeth's bed while she knelt to pray. Daddy, coming up the stairs, was outlined by the glow from the potbellied stove in the room below.

> *Now I lay me down to sleep.*
> *I pray the Lord my soul to keep.*
> *If I should die before I wake,*
> *I pray the Lord my soul to take.*

She took a breath. "God bless Mama and Daddy and Grandma and Grandpa and Uncle John and Annie and Sarah. And thank you, God, for Snowball. Amen."

Elizabeth climbed into her bed and pulled the patchwork quilt up to her chin. Then, remembering, she scrambled back out and dropped to her knees, clasping her hands tightly before her and squeezing her eyes shut.

"And God, please make Snowball's foot well."

Mama and Daddy looked at each other in surprise across her head.

Uncle John's bedroom was right beneath the girls'. It was an old house, and he heard Elizabeth's earnest prayer. His eyes glistened in the dark as he whispered, "Amen."

# Chapter 5

## *Up the Mountain*

*S*HE WAS BACK *in New Mexico, wearing her boots and red cowboy hat and walking through the desert with its hard, cracked earth. Yucca plants with their spiky leaves brushed against her jeans, and a tall cactus in front of her blossomed with yellow flowers. Up ahead a horned toad skittered under the edge of a boulder. She stooped down and peered at him, but he had turned into a coiled rattlesnake and shook his rattles at her.*

Elizabeth awoke with a start to the familiar bedroom. Just a dream, then. She curled around Annie, warm under the blankets, and started to slip back asleep.

Then she remembered. Grandpa was taking her up the mountain with him that day. They were going to haul down split rails for a new fence.

She scrambled out of bed and into her clothes and tiptoed down the stairs and through the darkened rooms to the kitchen.

Grandma was stuffing wood into the cookstove, and it was glowing, making the room toasty warm. A kerosene lantern with a sputtering wick on the small kitchen table was the only light. Elizabeth sat down, and Grandma began dishing up oatmeal, her eyes on Grandpa.

"John says it's fixin' to really rain," she said. Elizabeth paused with a spoonful of oatmeal halfway to her mouth. John talked to Grandma?

Grandpa went over to the high, small windows over the kitchen sink and looked out; then he went to open the back door and peer outside. A blast of cool, damp air curled around Elizabeth's ankles.

"It's always fixin' to rain here," he said, closing the door. "Work's gotta get done."

After breakfast they trudged up the hill to the barn where a small group of assorted uncles, cousins, and neighbors waited—all older, all men.

"You babysittin', Tom?" Don Miller laughed, scraping the mud off his boots with a stick.

Suddenly Elizabeth felt stupid. She slowed her steps and wished she were back in bed. Her cousin Clark, who was fifteen and proud to be going along, snorted.

Grandpa gave Elizabeth a leg up onto the driver's seat of the flatbed wagon and put the reins in her hands.

He turned to Clark. "Clarky, you step lively and get them horses."

Nobody said anything else about her coming along.

After Fanny and Maud were hitched up, the group crossed the stream between the farm and Tyler's Mountain. Grandpa drove the wagon through the water, and everyone else used the footbridge. Then the long trek up to the big timber began. Trees at the top had already been cut down and split several days before and just needed to be hauled down. There was heavy lifting ahead for the men.

Grandpa was driving most of the time, but every now and then he'd give the reins to Elizabeth and she'd take over, with him sitting right beside her. Mostly the horses just plodded ahead in the tracks up the hill, but Elizabeth pretended to guide them, jiggling the long reins on their backs and saying, "Giddyup." Sometimes she pulled the reins a little to the left and said, "Haw," raising her voice like Grandpa did, and sometimes she pulled on the right rein and shouted, "Gee!"

The horses' broad rumps swung to and fro. Maud's hair was chocolate brown, and Fanny's coat was white. Elizabeth had trouble believing that Fanny was Maud's mother, because they were the same size.

The road made by the tracks was narrow, just big enough for the wagon to pass, so the men walked ahead of the wagon going up the mountain and behind it coming down, in case it broke loose and went rolling.

The forest surrounded them—tall trees blotting out the sky, moss covering logs and rocks, ferns reaching out to brush the wagon as it passed. A Blue Jay flitted between two oaks. Ahead, the wagon tracks curved up the side of the mountain. The road was steep and went up into the clouds. Finally, though, they reached the clearing at the top, where logs lay all around.

Grandpa stopped the wagon at a pile that had been split longways. He and the other men began loading up the wagon. Elizabeth balanced on a big log, walking its length and pretending she was a tightrope walker in the circus.

At noon, she and Grandpa sat on a stump and ate lunch out of his tin—biscuits with thick slabs of cold bacon and a piece of apple pie each.

On the way back down, Grandpa had to use both hands to hold the brake handle in place so the wagon, heavy with wood, wouldn't push the horses. The muscles and veins in his arms stood out.

The woods were quiet. Too quiet. Then *boom!*— thunder followed by a flash of lightning. The horses jerked nervously. Elizabeth couldn't see their eyes because of the bridles' blinders, but she knew you could see the white parts.

Grandpa grabbed the reins and held them taut. "You're gonna have to walk," he said briskly. He was afraid the horses would run away.

Elizabeth walked beside Clark, who was being extra nice after that morning. They took turns kicking rocks over the edge of the mountain and watching them bounce far below.

It was pouring as they came to flatter land and reached the swollen stream close to home. Everyone walked single file across the footbridge. The water was so high it was washing over the planks. Clark took her hand as they picked their way across and held it so hard it hurt.

They stopped in a sodden group on the other side to watch Grandpa drive the horses and wagon through the swirling water. In the middle of the current, the water began to lift the wagon. Grandpa slapped the reins furiously. "Giddyup! Giddyup there!" The horses began to rear and thrash about in the foaming water as they were pulled downstream with the wagon.

"They'll drown!" Clark said in a frightened whisper. Elizabeth, scared and wet, wanted to cry. She didn't want Fanny and Maud to drown. Or Grandpa.

"Please, God," she whispered.

The men on the bank shouted and ran back and forth. Several started into the water.

"Get back!" Grandpa roared at them above the sound of the rushing water. Then he jumped from the wagon onto Maud's back, clinging to her mane. His knife flashed in his hand as he slashed the harness straps that held the doomed wagon to the horses and cut them free. They swam eagerly through the water toward the bank, Grandpa still on Maud, and clambered up onto the shore.

Clark grabbed Fanny and gentled her down. "It's OK. Easy girl."

On the bank everyone gathered around Grandpa, all talking at once, and stood and watched the wagon wash down the river.

Elizabeth sneezed, and suddenly the crowd parted and Grandpa strode toward her, taking off his heavy coat and putting it around her shoulders.

"Gotta get this girl inside before her Grandma kills me," he said to the men. Water poured off the brim of his hat. He hurried Elizabeth toward the house and the men followed more slowly—chatting in relief, anticipating coffee.

"Wait here," he said when they reached the back porch. "I'll get your Mama."

Elizabeth was shaking, and water dripped off her bangs and rolled down her nose. Suddenly she was aware of Uncle John, almost invisible in the false darkness of the storm, standing at the far end of the porch near the outside door to his room. An unspoken question hung in the air between them. Grandpa's courage had made Elizabeth brave—brave enough to speak to Uncle John.

"We're all OK!" Elizabeth shouted over the rain beating on the porch roof. "But we lost the wagon!"

Uncle John opened the door to his room and slipped silently inside.

Then the back door flew open, and Grandma and Mama were there with towels and fuss, and behind them the kerosene lamp flickered on the table, and the stove glowed and there was warmth and the smell of supper.

# Chapter 6

## *The Runaways*

MAMA WAS IN a bad mood. At breakfast each dish she set on the table made a *thump*.

*Thump*—biscuits with gravy.

*Thump*—fresh applesauce.

"What's the matter?" Daddy said.

"Nothing," Mama snapped. Then in a nicer voice, "I have a headache."

"Why don't you take it easy today?"

"I have too much to do," Mama sighed. "There's all that wash."

Elizabeth suddenly wondered if Mama missed her friends back in New Mexico and the adobe home they'd lived in for two years.

Annie ran into the backyard after breakfast to play, and Elizabeth followed her. She knew she'd have to help with the wash.

"You girls fetch some drinking water," Grandma called through the kitchen's screen door.

Elizabeth went back inside to get the water bucket, almost empty, and the large ladle. Annie was waiting at the back door, eager to help. Elizabeth let her hold onto the handle, and they made their way to the well.

Annie pumped the red-handled pump up and down until her little cheeks were pink but nothing came out.

"It has to be primed, silly," said Elizabeth. She carefully put the last of the water in the bucket into the ladle and poured it into the hole at the top of the pump, all the while executing short, vigorous pumps. The pump made a dry sucking sound like it was clearing its throat.

"Come on, come on," Elizabeth urged, just like Daddy always did. She had just recently learned to prime the pump and was proud of it.

"Come on!" Annie shouted, jumping up and down.

A trickle of water rewarded them. Elizabeth changed the tempo to slow, steady pumps of the long handle, and sparkling, clear water gushed out of the spout and into the waiting bucket.

"Yay!" squealed Annie, running around the yard in circles and then falling in the grass. Elizabeth laughed.

"You girls quiet down," Mama said crossly from the porch. She was dressed in a plaid, sleeveless shirt and denim pants rolled up to just below the knee. She had washed her hair and put it up in pin curls, a red-bandana kerchief tied around her head to keep the bobby pins in place. It was her wash-day outfit. Mama didn't wear pants unless she was washing all of her house dresses.

Mama came down and took the water bucket from under the pump and carried it inside, a little sloshing over the side. She came back with the wash bucket and started carting water from the rain barrel to fill the electric wringer washer that stood sturdily on its long metal legs on the back porch. Elizabeth grabbed a second bucket and dipped it in the rain barrel.

Elizabeth knew all about electricity from living in New Mexico, but Grandma and Grandpa had just had electricity put in the last summer, and it was like a miracle to them. Grandpa said it was unnatural and insisted on not using it most of the time—he still lit the kerosene lantern at dark. But on Saturday night he turned on the plastic radio and listened to country singin' and pickin', and Grandma listened to preaching on the gospel station when she had the time.

On wash day Mama loved electricity because she could use the washer instead of washing in a big tub with a washboard. After the clothes were washed, she turned the crank and ran them one at a time between the wooden wringers into a big tub of fresh water. She used a big stick to swish them around in the rinse water, and then moved the wringer and cranked them through again to squeeze the water out. This time they fell into a bushel basket that Mama lugged to the clothesline, where she hung them out to dry in the sun. Dark-colored clothes had to be turned inside out so the sun wouldn't fade them. Elizabeth loved to run between the lines of sweet-smelling sheets flapping on the line.

After the clothes were washed this morning, Elizabeth's job was to ease them through the wringer and into the rinse water.

"Careful and don't catch your fingers," Mama said.

There was her brown corduroy skirt intertwined with Annie's red sweater. She stirred them both in the rinse water with the other clothes. She wanted to show Annie, but her sister had gone to get the kittens from the box in the smokehouse.

"Annie, what are you doing?" Mama said sharply.

Annie was back at the pump. She had a small tabby kitten and was holding it under the dripping water. The kitten was sputtering and mewing weakly. Annie dropped the kitten and it tottered off.

"Just baptizin' Tiger, Mama."

Elizabeth laughed but Mama was not amused.

"Shame on you. You could drown the poor little thing. You know better than that!" She grabbed Annie's left arm and gave her a swat on her bottom. "You girls go play and leave me to my work."

Elizabeth took her sister's hand and led her around the house. Annie was going to cry—her mouth turned down in a pout, her hazel eyes welled with tears. Sometimes Annie was a pest. She was a tattletale. She copied everything Elizabeth did. When Elizabeth complained, Mama would just say, "She just wants to be like you, dear; it's a compliment." Some days Elizabeth didn't like Annie. But nobody, even Mama, should mistreat Annie. She put her arms around her little sister. She was mad at Mama. Annie didn't know any better—she was only four.

"Don't cry, Annie."

Suddenly she got an idea. It was from a book she had borrowed from the bookmobile, which labored up the hill once a month with the seats removed and bookcases lining the walls. "I know!" she said triumphantly. "We'll run away from home!"

Annie stopped crying and looked interested.

"We'll pack the dolls and some food, and we'll run away!" Elizabeth leaped to her feet.

Annie jumped up too. "Run away!" she said, clapping her hands.

Elizabeth went into the kitchen. Because it was ten in the morning, no one was there, but the stove was still warm from breakfast. Grandma would be starting dinner in another hour.

She'd assigned Annie the task of packing up the dolls, telling her carefully which two to take and what clothes to pack for them. She was going to pack some food; she had learned that much from the library book.

Elizabeth opened the pantry door and chose a paper bag from the stack folded neatly on the lower shelf. The pantry looked like a big clothes closet, except there were shelves all the way to the ceiling on either side, stocked with canned fruits and vegetables in glass jars—things like peaches and green beans and apple butter. On the floor was a wooden bin where Grandma stored potatoes.

On the shelf just above Elizabeth's head were a box of corn flakes, a round box of oatmeal, a jar of store-bought peanut butter, and a jar of blackberry jelly from Aunt Luella. She carefully lifted the two jars down. Then she got a table knife out of the drawer and split open two biscuits, spreading them with peanut butter and jelly. The biscuits crumbled a bit, and she licked off the crumbs that stuck to the knife.

Hurrying, afraid she'd be discovered, she wrapped the biscuits in waxed paper and put them in the bag, cleaned up, and headed for the side porch where she'd told Annie to meet her.

Everyone was out working, and the house was empty. She saw a pile of dirty clothes on the bedroom floor as she passed by. Inspired, she veered off into the bedroom and got them each a sweater out of the drawer and snagged Annie's blanket.

"Blanket!" Annie said joyously. Elizabeth threw it to her and picked up her doll Molly and a paper bag full of doll clothes. "C'mon."

Grandma had made Molly for her when she was little, and Elizabeth still loved her. She was a biscuit-head doll because Grandma had cut around the biscuit cutter to shape her head. Her hair was reddish-brown yarn, and her eyes and mouth were carefully stitched with embroidery thread—big blue eyes wide open with lots of lashes and permanently surprised brows, two little black dots for nostrils, and a red bow mouth. She was dressed in the blue-flowered dress with a white apron that she had on when Elizabeth found her under the Christmas tree.

Elizabeth went across the side porch with its two big swings at either end, through the yard, and out the gate, with Annie trailing behind.

Annie was carrying her blanket and Lulu. She had gotten Lulu for Christmas the same year Elizabeth had gotten Molly. Elizabeth liked Lulu better than Molly, but she didn't tell anyone. She wished Lulu had been for her. Lulu had yarn hair that could be braided or gathered at the back of her neck into a bun. She was made like Molly, but her head wasn't quite so flat. She was prettier, Elizabeth thought.

They were halfway up the hill to the barn.

"Lulu's tired," Annie said. "And she wants her sunbonnet on."

"Let's wait until we get to the big tree." Elizabeth pointed to the giant oak by the barn.

Annie whined a little.

"You know what, Annie? We can have a picnic!"

Annie perked up and held her doll up in front of her face, "Know what, Lulu? We can have a picnic!"

When they got to the shade of the tree, Elizabeth spread out Annie's blanket, and they both settled down, spread out the doll clothes, and opened up the lunch bag. Elizabeth carefully peeled back the waxed paper and took out a biscuit, dripping jelly. She and Annie had one each. They tasted lovely but were messy.

Elizabeth wiped her hands on the grass. Annie had peanut butter and jelly on her cheeks and had spilled some jelly on her blanket. They were both thirsty, and Elizabeth had forgotten water. "Come on," she said brightly. "We can wash your face in the cow's trough."

They went through the cool interior of the barn. All the animals had been let out to graze on the hillside. Around the corner of the barn was the big metal trough, so tall Annie could just peek over the edge. They washed and splashed and took a drink. Daddy would have told them only to drink well water, but they didn't care. It was a warm day and they were running away, after all. They didn't have to do what Mama and Daddy said.

Now they were damp and tired.

"I want Blanket," Annie said. She was crabby, and Elizabeth was tired of taking care of her.

They went back around the barn and saw in dismay that two cows were milling around under the tree. Belle was munching grass, but White Face was snuffling around on Annie's blanket.

"Blanket!" Annie screamed and went running toward them. White Face was startled. Her eyes got big, and she rolled them around. Then she turned and faced the girls and lowered her head. The stubs of her horns gleamed in the sunlight. She started plodding toward Annie, swinging her head from side to side. Something red was in her mouth. It was a doll's dress.

Elizabeth ran forward and grabbed Annie's arm and pulled her into the barn. "C'mon—she's mad."

White Face was still coming—the big bell around her neck clanging gently.

"*Moooooo*," Belle said and followed White Face.

Suddenly, Uncle John was there. He grabbed Annie and hoisted her up into the hayloft above his head, not even taking time for the ladder nailed flush to the wall.

Elizabeth was so surprised to see him that she froze with her mouth open, not even moving when he motioned to her urgently. Just as she felt the cow's hot breath on her back, Uncle John took two quick strides toward her, grabbed her arm, and boosted her up the ladder.

From the safety of the opening to the loft, Elizabeth watched with a dry mouth as he turned to face the cows. There wasn't time for him to climb to safety, so he spread his arms wide and stood completely still.

White Face lowered her head and Elizabeth held her breath, afraid she would gore him. Instead the cow snuffled at his shirt front, leaving a slimy trail with her nose. Then she hesitated, turned aside, grabbed a mouthful of hay that had tumbled out of the loft and began to chew loudly. As soon as White Face lost interest, Belle did too, wandering back out into the sunlight.

Behind Elizabeth, Annie started crying for her blanket. Elizabeth crawled over to her across the hay. "It'll be OK," Elizabeth assured her. "They'll be going down for evening milkin' soon, and we'll go get Blanket." When she looked out again, the cows were gone and Uncle John was gone.

"Thank you," Elizabeth whispered into the darkness of the barn.

The sisters lay on their backs in the hay and watched a yellow jacket butting his head on the ceiling high above them. Annie whimpered a bit.

"Lizzie, will he sting us?" Annie was afraid of wasps. So was Elizabeth but she pretended she wasn't. "He can't see us from up there," she said reassuringly.

They watched the rays of the sun come in through the boards and light up dust particles floating in the air. Everything had a hazy, golden glow. Elizabeth's eyelids drooped.

Suddenly she woke with a start—someone was whistling. Annie was snuggled up against her.

Daddy peeked over the edge of the loft. "Anybody home?" he said cheerfully.

Elizabeth and Annie scrambled to the edge, and Daddy helped them down. They had hay in their hair.

Mama was coming up the hill with Sarah on her hip. Her hair was combed out into golden-brown curls, and she was wearing a soft blue dress. Sarah was only wearing a diaper and her skin was creamy white. The sun's fading rays bathed them both in pinkish-gold light.

"Lithie, Lithie," Sarah said, stretching out her pudgy little arms. Elizabeth took her and kissed her round cheek.

Mama stooped down and put her arms around Annie. "I'm sorry I was a grouch," she said. Then she smiled up at Elizabeth.

Suddenly Annie remembered. "White Face ate the doll clothes," she said excitedly. "And Blanket!"

"They're all right here." Daddy leaned over to pick up the scattered belongings.

"White Face chased us," Elizabeth said, looking straight at Daddy. "Uncle John scared her away."

Daddy's head jerked up. "John?" he said in surprise.

Mama looked concerned. "Praise the Lord for Uncle John," she said.

Annie buried her nose in her blanket and then went through the doll clothes. "White Face ate Lulu's red dress," she declared, looking like she might cry once more.

"I'll make you another," Mama said, giving her a squeeze. She took Sarah back and walked down the hill with Daddy. Annie and Elizabeth followed.

"If White Face has a baby," Annie whispered loudly to Elizabeth, "it will come out in Lulu's red dress."

Elizabeth started to tell her that was silly, but then the image of a calf wearing a red dress popped into her mind. She started to snicker, and then Annie giggled too. Hearing them, Sarah bounced up and down in Mama's arms and clapped her hands together, which made everyone laugh. Their laughter drifted out over the golden hills.

That night, even though it was only Wednesday and there was only dessert on Sunday, Mama had made a huckleberry pie. When Uncle John came out of his room for supper, there was an extra large piece sitting on one of the good dishes by his place.

And he ate it first, before supper, and nobody said a word about it.

# Chapter 7

## *Haying with Patsy*

F OR THE SEVENTH time Elizabeth rounded the corner of the barn and skipped to the edge of the hill so she could see down the valley. The dusty road below followed the shape of the mountain.

She was waiting for Cousin Patsy because that day Grandpa was going to put up hay and she and Patsy were going to help. Patsy's father was Uncle Dan, Daddy's brother, who was a coal miner. Every night after work, he was covered with soot and had to bathe in a tub out in the shed before Aunt Gladys would let him in the house. He had worked in the mines so long that he coughed a lot from the coal dust.

Daddy and Grandpa were in the barn hitching up Fanny and Maud to the rake. Elizabeth was dividing her time between watching them and keeping an eye out for Patsy. On her next trip back from the barn, she was rewarded when an old Ford pickup pulled into sight, followed by a cloud of dust. Patsy got out, her chestnut hair lighting up in the sunlight.

Elizabeth waved wildly. "Up here! We're up here!"

Patsy started up the hill at a run, climbing effortlessly and leaving Uncle Dan to plod along behind.

Elizabeth loved Cousin Patsy. She had fair skin like Elizabeth that freckled across her nose and down her arms in the sun. She liked to be outdoors and around the animals and climb trees. She was thirteen, but being a teenager hadn't spoiled her.

Patsy and Elizabeth stood grinning at each other.

"C'mon." Patsy grabbed her hand and they ran to the barn, just as Grandpa came out leading the horses who were pulling the rake. The front part of the rake looked just like a wagon with a seat for the driver, but in the back there was no wagon bed, just the giant curved teeth. A big handle allowed the driver to lower the comb so it could rake up the hay.

"Hullo, Patricia Sue," Grandpa said.

"Can we ride Fanny and Maud, Grandpa?" Patsy said breathlessly.

"Not just yet, girl."

Uncle Dan bit off a piece of tobacco and worked the "chaw" into his cheek. He spit sideways.

"We best get started," he said.

The little party proceeded to the edge of the hill. Below them spread the lower meadow. The hay that had grown steadily into a tall, wavy sea of grass had been cut weeks ago and left to dry in the summer sun. Aunt Luella's five boys, who lived past Calvin, had spent one day turning it with pitchforks so the underside could dry. Now it was ready to be put into haystacks so the cows and horses would have something to eat through the cold winter months.

It was only eight o'clock, but Elizabeth could already feel the hot sun on her bare arms as they moved down into the meadow.

First Grandpa lowered the teeth of the rake and clicked to the horses to "Giddyup." They knew just what to do and walked steadily ahead gathering up the dried hay behind them.

Elizabeth and Patsy weren't needed yet. They sat in the shade of a tree making daisy chains. Patsy knew just how to wind them together so they wouldn't break. She made a daisy crown for herself and one for Elizabeth, then carefully selected a daisy and plucked the petals one by one.

"He loves me. He loves me not."

Elizabeth watched in surprise. "Patricia Sue, do you have a boyfriend?" she blurted out. She hoped not. She didn't want Patsy to change and be like her older sister, who was girlish and wore perfume that made Elizabeth sneeze.

"Maybe. Maybe not." Patsy grabbed her hand. "C'mon."

They ran through the fields disturbing the grasshoppers, who flew ahead of them by the hundreds. Patsy caught one and held it against her thumb and they chanted, "Spit tobacco, spit tobacco, spit tobacco, SPIT!" The frightened grasshopper deposited a black droplet on Patsy's thumb.

"Yuk," Elizabeth said, and Patsy threw the grasshopper up in the air and he flew away.

They ran down to the little creek that trickled through the meadow to search for crayfish. Some people said crayfish looked like tiny lobsters but Elizabeth had never seen a lobster. She pulled off her boots and waded into the water, which was warm from the sun, turning over rocks. Suddenly under a big, flat rock she spied a crayfish, who scrambled desperately to get away. She plunged her hand into the water, caught him behind his pinchers, and held him aloft for Patsy to see.

"Yahoo! Got one!"

Patsy had a long stem of timothy grass in her mouth and was lying on the bank staring up at the blue sky. Elizabeth let the crayfish go and dropped down beside her. She had been wanting to ask Patsy *the question* and maybe this was the time.

"What do you think is wrong with Uncle John?" she asked earnestly.

Patsy rolled on her side and looked at Elizabeth, her eyes sparkling. She knew this was a taboo subject—it was almost like a secret and Patsy loved secrets.

"Maybe he was dropped on his head when he was a baby," she laughed. Then catching the look on Elizabeth's face, she fell silent.

"He's just strange, that's all," she said tossing her hair.

"He is not!" Elizabeth said hotly. "He's smart and talented and kind and I don't know why no one likes him."

"What do you care? Just stay away from him," Patsy said, surprised by the outburst.

"I don't *want* to stay away from him. I want, I want . . ."

"Well what *do* you want?" Patsy asked, intrigued.

"I want people to talk to him. I want him to be part of the family. I want to be his friend." Elizabeth was startled to feel tears prick her eyes.

"Well, what are you going to do about it?" Patsy was pushing.

"I don't know—but *something*," Elizabeth sniffed.

Patsy stood and brushed the seat of her pants. "Well, good luck with that. Hey, Lizette, want to climb The Tree?" *Lizette* was Patsy's pet name for her. Mama didn't like it; she said it was *fresh* and *sassy* so Patsy only used it when they were alone.

"The Tree" was the giant pine at the edge of the woods. It was cooler in the woods and small white flowers, ferns, and tiny plants covered the forest floor. Big fallen logs were covered with moss.

"Look, shhhhh." A doe stood frozen on the far bank, her coat red-brown with white spots. Suddenly she flipped up her white tail and bounded off.

They stopped at the spring bubbling out of the mountain to get an ice-cold drink. Finally they reached the base of the pine.

"I'll give you a leg up." Patsy locked her hands in stirrup position under the tree.

Elizabeth did as she was told, hanging onto Patsy's hair and suddenly was boosted up into the sweet-smelling evergreen.

She grabbed the nearest branch and clambered up. "Now me. Look out."

Patsy leaped and caught a branch and swung her legs over another. She let go with her hands and hung upside down, her shirt hanging down over her face.

"Try it," she dared Elizabeth.

Elizabeth hesitated. It was a long way down.

"Scaredy-cat!" Patsy taunted.

Elizabeth carefully lowered herself, then let go and swung, clinging with her knees. Her pigtails hung down beside her head and her heart hammered against her chest.

"OK, let's get to work." Patsy was satisfied and started climbing the tree.

They had been working on that tree all summer, clearing tiny, dead branches out all the way to the top. Eventually it would be a clean climb. They easily climbed up to where they had stopped last time and then had to start snapping off branches again, watching them fall down below.

They worked steadily without speaking for a while. Then . . .

"Paaatsyyy . . . Eliiiizabethhh . . ." It was Daddy calling.

Patsy wrinkled up her nose and made a face.

"Haystack time," she groaned.

Going down was faster than coming up.

"Where are your boots?" Daddy said.

Elizabeth went tearing back to the riverbank.

Grandpa had raked the hay into little stacks all over the field. He had unhitched the horses from the rake and now had each one pulling the small stacks toward the six tall, heavy poles dotting the meadow.

Daddy and Uncle Dan were piling the hay at the base of the first pole, walking around and around, packing and shaping the hay. Daddy got on top of the pile and stamped it down. Pretty soon the hay was halfway up the pole, above the men's heads.

"OK, girls. Your turn."

Patsy was handed up to the top of the growing stack. She held onto the pole and leaned down for Elizabeth, who scrambled up.

"Tromp it down good, girls."

Elizabeth and Patsy kept their right hand on the pole and stomped steadily around it following each other. The men hoisted up more hay with pitchforks, being careful not to stab the girls.

As the haystack curved gracefully in, only Elizabeth was left on the top to pack in the last little bit. Then she sat down and slid to the ground.

At lunchtime, they had two stacks done. Patsy and Elizabeth compared sunburns. Mama, who had walked down with a picnic basket and a jug of lemonade, made them put on men's long-sleeved shirts and some old straw hats to protect them from the sun.

At the end of the day, all six stacks were spaced across the field, graceful as if smoothed by a sculptor's hand. The setting sun turned them all orange-red on one side.

As a reward, Patsy was boosted up on Maud's back and Elizabeth on Fanny's as the tired horses were led to the barn and their stalls.

"Well, I know two girls who Snowball, Fanny, and Maud will be mighty grateful to, come January," Grandpa said.

"And White Face and Belle," Elizabeth said.

"And Petunia and Patrick the Mule," Patsy added.

They grinned at each other. Patsy had freckles all over her face and arms. Elizabeth had hay sticking in her hair. They were proud of their job—the men couldn't have done it without them.

Elizabeth looked down at Daddy and Grandpa and Uncle Dan walking beside them. They weren't so big after all.

Fanny's back was so broad that Elizabeth could just get her legs around her. Then she fell backwards, lying with her head on the horse's broad rump, and looked up at the moon making its faint appearance, lulled by the horse's gentle plodding.

# Chapter 8

## *Patrick the Mule*

I T WAS PLANTING time, and Elizabeth went up to the north pasture with Grandpa to help out. After he was done plowing, she was going to fill her apron with corn and follow him down the rows, dropping the hard kernels carefully into the waiting earth. In late summer they'd have corn on the cob every day, Grandma said.

For now, Elizabeth made herself comfortable under a shade tree while Grandpa hitched up Patrick the Mule to the rusty old plow.

"Giddyup," Grandpa said, making a clicking noise with his tongue and slapping the long reins against Patrick's back.

Patrick didn't move.

Elizabeth watched with interest. Who would win? Patrick or Grandpa?

Everyone said that mules were stubborn. Mama called Elizabeth stubborn when she refused to drink the last of her milk. *Stubborn* meant you didn't do what someone else wanted you to do no matter how much they tried to make you. Patrick didn't feel like plowing the field. He felt like cocking his back hoof, letting his head droop, and closing his eyes.

Patrick still hadn't moved and Grandpa was getting red in the face. Elizabeth got to her feet.

"Grandpa, what's wrong?" she shouted, cupping her hands around her mouth.

"This durn mule's balking," he called back.

Elizabeth left the coolness of the tree and made her way through the stubble from last year's corn stalks to Grandpa and Patrick.

Grandpa pulled the reins over Patrick's head and handed them to Elizabeth. "You pull and I'll push," he said, going around behind Patrick.

Sometimes animals kicked, and Elizabeth knew you had to be careful going behind them. Grandma always told the story of second-cousin Elmer, who was kicked in the head by a horse and died. "Sophie's boy," Grandma would say, wiping tears from her soft, crinkly cheeks. "God rest his soul."

But Patrick had never kicked. Grandpa put his back against Patrick's rump and pushed with all his might.

"Now pull!" he yelled up to Elizabeth, short of breath from the effort.

Elizabeth pulled on Patrick's reins with all of her strength. She dug her bare feet into the dirt and leaned back so her pigtails swung free behind her.

Patrick stretched out his long neck with its scraggly mane that stood straight up like a black scrub brush. He extended his long brown muzzle. He opened up his mouth and jutted his lower jaw sideways and showed his big square yellow teeth. He rolled his eyes and showed their whites, and he laid back his ears. He stood like his four legs were tree trunks growing up out of the ground.

Elizabeth leaned back so far that she sat down *pouf* in the dirt.

Grandpa came around from behind Patrick. His shirt was wet and clinging to him. He took off his hat and threw it on the ground. "Dang!" he said.

Elizabeth sat quietly on the ground in front of Patrick. She held onto the reins. Patrick didn't look like he was going to run away, but you just never knew with a mule. She wondered if Grandpa was going to hit Patrick.

Grandpa took out a red bandana handkerchief and wiped the sweat off his neck and face. He took a plug of tobacco out of his pocket and bit off a wad.

Elizabeth's heart began to flutter in her chest like a frightened bird, but she couldn't stop the words.

"Uncle John could help," she said in a rush.

Grandpa glared at her. He took the reins and squatted down next to the mule. Patrick gazed off into the blue distance placidly.

"Go git him," he said finally.

Elizabeth went flying down the hill, bare feet pounding on the grass. Chickens were pecking up grain that Grandma had scattered in front of the granary, but Elizabeth didn't slow down.

"Braaaack!" squawked a rooster in alarm when he saw her coming. Elizabeth ran right through the chickens, and they scattered in all directions, flapping and clucking in terror.

Grandma stuck her head out the granary door. "Elizabeth Rose, sake's alive!"

"Where's Uncle John?" Elizabeth said breathlessly.

"He's in the coal house. What's the matter?"

"Patrick's gone stubborn," Elizabeth called over her shoulder.

The coal house was a small outbuilding behind the main farmhouse but inside the fenced-in yard. Once a month a truck trundled up the hill, backed up carefully to the large, open window on the side, and dumped an avalanche of black, glistening coal into the little building until it seemed about to burst. Elizabeth always ran out to watch the driver shovel the last of the load on top of the pile, his face and clothing covered with coal dust.

Once a day, the big metal coal bucket in the house had to be filled so that it was there to shovel into the fireplace in the living room and into the potbellied stove in the upper room to keep them warm. Elizabeth found Uncle John shoveling coal and muttering to himself. He didn't look up. His soft cloth shirt was damp against his back. A lock of dark hair fell across his forehead.

Elizabeth was suddenly shy. The silence between her and Uncle John was broken only by the sound of Uncle John's shovel and Elizabeth's heavy breathing. "It's Patrick," she finally blurted out.

Uncle John carefully finished filling the coal bucket. Then he carried it into the house, staggering under its weight. He came back out, adjusting his suspenders and dusting his hands. He didn't look at her or say anything, just started up the hill to the upper pasture. She ran along behind.

Patrick was dozing in the warm sun. Grandpa had moved over into the shade. He spit sideways and a black stream of tobacco shot out and landed in a little glistening puddle in the grass. Elizabeth joined him.

Uncle John walked softly across the hardened earth straight to Patrick. He stretched his hand out before him, palm up. Patrick looked up with interest and nickered softly. When John began to stroke his neck, the mule curved his head around sideways and snuffled in his pockets. John produced a carrot, and Patrick munched it eagerly.

Now John was murmuring in one of Patrick's long, soft ears.

"What's he saying?" Elizabeth whispered to Grandpa.

"Lord only knows." Grandpa had a hayseed stalk sticking out of his mouth.

Then John patted Patrick on the shoulder and walked away over the edge of the hill toward the house. Patrick watched him until he was out of sight.

Elizabeth was disappointed. Patrick was still standing like he was rooted to the ground.

Grandpa took a big drink of water from the canteen Uncle Joe had brought him back from the war. His Adam's apple went up and down as he drank, and water trickled down his chin and neck and wet his shirt. He screwed the lid closed and put his hat back on. Then he marched across the field to Patrick, positioned himself behind the plow, and took up the reins. "Gee up there!" he called to Patrick.

Patrick moved ahead obediently. His long ears were forward, giving him an eager look. The sharp blade of the plow split the brown earth behind him.

Elizabeth stood with her mouth open and watched. She expected Patrick to stop any minute and not move again.

But he didn't.

*Maybe it was the carrot*, she thought.

But she knew it wasn't the carrot. Grandpa knew it too.

# Chapter 9

## *Vacation Bible School*

IT WAS TIME for vacation Bible school at Alderson Baptist Church, and Elizabeth was excited. She would go in the school-age class, and Annie would go with Mama, who was teaching the little kids. Sarah was too little and stayed home with Grandma.

The first day started with everyone chanting the books of the Bible along with Miss Pritchard.

"Genesis, Exodus, Leviticus . . ."

It reminded Elizabeth of school. She remembered all the daydreaming she had done in New Mexico about the little white clapboard school back in the mountains. She couldn't wait to go back in the fall. Her thoughts went spinning off.

She noticed that the Caldwells from down the holler were barefoot. She knew Gary Caldwell because he had been in her class before they went to New

Mexico. He was the oldest of six brothers and sisters and was always having to mind them for his mama. She knew his younger brother Norman too. Norman was in kindergarten, and when the rickety yellow bus had come to pick her up down by the road in the winter, the Caldwells were already crowded three to a seat and Norman was crying. He cried because he was cold. He cried because he was hungry.

"Numbers, Deuteronomy, Joshua . . ."

Two weeks ago Sunday, Daddy had suggested an afternoon ride in the car, and Mama had pointed out the Caldwells' house. It wasn't much more than a shed with a crooked screen door and chickens walking around in the yard. A rusty old Chevrolet with the tires off was at the side of the house with wildflowers growing up through the windows.

Daddy said the Caldwells should know better than to dump their trash in the creek, but Mama was sorry for them. She said times were hard and Mr. Caldwell hadn't worked for a long time and she didn't know how Mrs. Caldwell managed with six children. In August, when there were extra vegetables from the garden, more than could be canned, Mama always filled a gunny sack with corn and tomatoes and asked Uncle John to take it to the Caldwells.

"Judges, Ruth, Samuel One and Two . . ."

Cassie Fletcher, across the table from Elizabeth, opened her mouth wide when she recited. Her brother

Roger was too old to come to Bible school. In the winter the Fletchers rode the school bus too. They lived in a tumbledown shack across the river from the hard road. Mr. Fletcher drank, and Mrs. Fletcher had run off.

Each morning the school bus came down the road and stopped and waited across the river from the Fletcher house. Cassie and Roger had to cross the river in an old rowboat, trying to get there in time for the bus. Usually they were late, and everyone sat in the bus and watched them rowing across. In the dead of winter, when the river was partially frozen, it took them longer. Roger would stand up in the boat breaking the ice with an oar while Cassie rowed from the back of the boat. In the afternoon going home, they had to break the ice all over again. Sometimes in the spring the river was so swollen that it was dangerous for them to try to cross, and they missed school. Sometimes the river flooded the road and then everyone got a vacation day.

"Kings One and Two, Chronicles One and Two, Ezra, Nehemiah, Esther, Job, Psalms!"

Elizabeth blinked. The class had stopped reciting—they only had to say up to Psalms today—and everyone was being given a picture with a verse to learn. Elizabeth's picture was of Jesus holding a lamb. Birds were flying around his head, and sheep were gathered at his feet. He had a tall staff with a curve at the top. Across the bottom the verse read, "The Lord Is My Shepherd."

Bessie Evans, Doc Evans' daughter and the most popular girl in school, had a picture of Jesus sitting down with children crowding around and one sitting in his lap. It said, "Suffer the Little Children to Come Unto Me." Elizabeth didn't know why it said *suffer*. Were the children suffering like Norman did on the school bus on winter mornings?

Then came a snack—cookies the mothers had brought in and cherry Kool-Aid that gave all the children red moustaches. Elizabeth recognized Grandma's buttermilk cookies in with the others.

Then they moved together up the stairs that came out at the back of the sanctuary, Miss Pritchard saying "Shhh, shhh," and out the door into the bright sunlight. They made a circle on the green grass under a big oak tree and played games.

During "The Farmer in the Dell," Elizabeth got to be the cat in the center. The children circled around, all eyes on her, singing:

> *The cat takes a rat,*
> *The cat takes a rat,*
> *Heigh-ho, the derry-o,*
> *The cat takes a rat.*

She picked Bessie to come into the center and be the rat. She couldn't pick a boy, although boys made the best rats, because then everyone would say she was sweet on him. Then Mama's class came out. Elizabeth held Annie's hand and circled, singing:

> *Ring around the rosie,*
> *Pocket full of posies,*
> *Ashes, ashes,*
> *We all . . . fall . . . down!*

At the last line, the children tumbled on the grass, laughing. Elizabeth pulled handfuls of grass and threw them at everyone and up in the air. Afterwards, they were told to sit quietly in a circle and wait for Rev. John Brown to come and say a prayer over them.

Uncle John was named for Rev. Brown, who was Grandma's brother, but they weren't at all alike as far as Elizabeth was concerned. Rev. Brown was fierce looking, with frizzy gray hair that stood out from his head in a halo. He had a bushy gray beard that reached all the way to his belt in front and he was always dressed in a worn black suit.

He used to be a circuit rider, back when most of the towns didn't even have a church. He rode his big bay horse from town to town, preaching the gospel, performing weddings and baptisms, burying people, and staying with the mountain folk for weeks at a time before moving on. Grandma said it was a hard life that had made him gruff. He had settled down when the community got together and built Alderson Baptist Church.

"Does anyone have any questions about the Lord?" he growled out at the children.

No one said anything. Everyone was afraid of him. Elizabeth felt someone should say something. She raised her hand, and Rev. Brown raised his eyebrows.

"Elizabeth Rose?"

Rev. Brown always used both of her names. Her middle name was Grandma's first name and Elizabeth was proud she had Grandma's name. "If God is our *other* father," she said, "then who is our *other* mother?" It was something she had been mulling over for some time.

Rev. Brown had never been asked that question before. If he had been Catholic, he probably would have said the Blessed Virgin Mary, the mother of Jesus. But Rev. Brown was Bible Baptist.

The children held their breath, looking sideways at Elizabeth in awe.

"The church is, child. The church is our other mother."

Elizabeth didn't see how a building could be a mother.

"Come walk with me, young'un."

Now Elizabeth wished she had kept quiet. Rev. Brown moved off through the graveyard, and she followed reluctantly, reading tombstones as she went. She knew where her family's section of the cemetery was. Uncle Dan's stillborn son was buried there, and

Grandma's sister Zanna. Great-grandma and Great-grandpa McCreary had fresh flowers on their graves.

Elizabeth heard the children playing "Mother, May I?" Bessie was the mother.

"Mother, may I take a giant step?" Gary Caldwell shouted.

"Yes, you may," Bessie called back primly.

"Elizabeth Rose, how old are you now?" the pastor asked.

"I'm eleven."

"I understand from your grandma that you ain't never been baptized."

"Yes, sir. That's right." Elizabeth felt something like fear in her stomach.

"I'm holding a service down at the river on Sunday—baptizing sinners. Do you know you're a sinner, Elizabeth Rose?"

Elizabeth thought about her sins. Sometimes she got mad at Annie. That must be what he meant. She nodded her head.

"Praise the Lord. I'm gonna talk to your folks about you being baptized come Sunday—joining the ranks of the faithful. God bless you." And he moved off.

There was a big discussion at home over dinner about the baptism. Daddy, who only went to church on Christmas and Easter, didn't like the idea. He didn't like Rev. Brown, even if he was Grandma's brother. "I don't want her head filled with that religious hogwash," he said a little too loudly.

Grandpa shoveled in the mashed potatoes and didn't say anything. He knew better than to cross Grandma, and Grandma was bound and determined Elizabeth should be baptized.

"Supposin' she should die," she said to Daddy. "The Bible says no one shall enter the pearly gates except they be born again. You want her to get to heaven, don't you?"

Daddy's mouth was set in a hard line. He appealed to Mama. "What do you think, Katie?"

Mama looked thoughtful. "I was baptized when I was her age," she said. "And Jesus was baptized."

Grandma nodded vigorously.

Daddy was feeling besieged. "Pa?" he said, looking for help.

"Leave me out of it," Grandpa said. "The women gotta have their religion."

Daddy turned to Elizabeth. "Lizzie, what do you think? You don't have to do this, you know."

There was a silence, and everyone looked at Elizabeth. She felt important. She looked at Annie, who didn't like supper and was having two peanut butter sandwiches instead. She was eating the insides of the sandwiches and leaving the crusts, piling them in a neat little stack beside her plate. Elizabeth hated it when she wouldn't eat her supper and begged for peanut butter sandwiches. She hated the way she piled up her crusts. Could it be she hated Annie? Maybe she did need her sins washed away.

Also, she wanted to go to heaven, which had streets of gold and soft green grass and lambs and angels and lots of candy, according to Bessie Evans. She couldn't really imagine a place better than Grandma's farm, except for the candy part. But Jesus was there, and he was just the nicest person ever.

She narrowed her eyes and looked at Uncle John, having cornbread spread with applesauce at the end of the table. "Was Uncle John baptized?" she asked.

There was a dead silence in the room. Uncle John didn't look up but stopped chewing mid-bite.

Grandma finally spoke. "Well, yes, of course," she said. "He was right about your age too."

"Then I'll do it," Elizabeth said.

Daddy looked at John, who had resumed chewing, and then he sighed and pushed his chair back from the table. "All right. I give up."

Grandma gave Elizabeth a big hug.

The next Sunday after services, Elizabeth was on the banks of Beaver Creek along with the congregation of Alderson Baptist Church. She was dressed in a flowered cotton dress that Grandma had cut down from one she found in Aunt Lorena's closet. Her hair was in braids so it wouldn't get in her eyes when it got wet. She was barefoot, and the little stones at the edge of the water hurt her feet.

She scanned the riverbank, searching all the faces. The ladies on the shore were fanning themselves fervently. They wore big hats to shade them from the sun.

"Elizabeth Rose McCreary," Rev. Brown's voice boomed. He was in the middle of the river dressed in his suit. He held out his hand to her, and several people helped her wade out into the water.

Soon she and the preacher were standing in water up to Elizabeth's armpits. Rev. Brown had his arm around her shoulders and his eyes shut with his head tilted back and his face pointed heavenward. He was praying loudly over her, but Elizabeth was so scared she didn't hear a word. She was shivering all over, even though it was mid-summer. She saw Mama and Grandma's faces back on the shore. Grandma was dabbing at her eyes with a handkerchief.

"Glory to God, glory to God, glory to God," Elizabeth kept whispering over and over to herself, afraid she'd forget. Grandma had told her that was what to say when she came up out of the water.

Suddenly Rev. Brown's arm tightened, and before Elizabeth could even think, he dipped her backwards and under the water, and there was no sound and then she was up out of the water again, coughing. And through her wet eyelashes, she saw who she'd been looking for—Uncle John standing apart from the crowd but watching nevertheless.

"Glory to God," Elizabeth whispered, her eyes fixed on him.

Then she was climbing back up the bank, and someone put a towel around her, and Grandma was there with tears in her old blue eyes and a big smile, promising Elizabeth a new white Bible of her very own waiting back at home.

# Chapter 10

## *Trip to Craigsville*

ELIZABETH WAS GOING with Grandpa to Craigsville to get a new bit for Maud's bridle—the bit went in the horse's mouth so the rider could steer. She was excited because Grandpa sometimes bought her an ice cream at Ruby's Drug Store.

Grandpa made homemade ice cream several times each summer. He would haul out the big wooden bucket with a crank and fill it with chopped ice sprinkled with salt to make it even colder. Inside the bucket of ice and attached to a handle was a smaller metal container that Grandma filled with milk straight from Petunia, mixed with sugar and crushed berries or peaches. Everyone took turns cranking the handle and spinning the silver-colored container. It took a long time. Then Grandpa would open the lid and there, like magic, would be delicious ice cream.

Elizabeth's favorite was raspberry, which Grandma usually made for Daddy's birthday in July. Grandpa didn't like raspberry because he wore false teeth and the little seeds would get stuck in them.

But the ice cream at Ruby's was like nothing Elizabeth had ever tasted—so smooth it was like licking satin. And there was chocolate, which they couldn't make at home, and it was in cones.

They were climbing into the old black Chevy when Mama came running out of the house, her purse over one arm.

"Looks like you're goin' along," said Grandpa.

"Rose has come up with a grocery list," Mama said.

Elizabeth was disappointed that Mama was coming. Maybe she wouldn't want her to have ice cream. She'd say, "Oh, she doesn't need that stuff" or "It's too expensive" or "We can make it at home." Also, Elizabeth had wanted to ride in the front seat with Grandpa, and now she had to sit in the back.

She could see Mama had changed her dress for the trip into town and brushed her flyaway brown curls and put on some lipstick, a little of which she had smeared on her fingertips and smoothed on her cheeks for rouge.

Elizabeth thought Mama looked odd with makeup on, like one of those store-bought dolls, but Grandpa smiled at her. "Well, aren't you all gussied up!"

Mama's dimples showed and her face got pink.

They jounced along. Elizabeth got on her knees facing backwards and looked out the back window at the cloud of dust behind them as the old car jolted over the ruts in the farm road.

Grandpa didn't drive very often, and he clutched the wheel and squinted into the distance. At the bottom of the hill, he stopped and slowly looked both ways, took a deep breath, and pulled onto the hard road.

The hard road was so smooth that it reminded Elizabeth of sledding on an old inner tube on the snow-covered hills in winter. She pretended that she was on a magic carpet, like in *Aladdin and the Magic Lamp*, flying over the mountains.

"Oh, look, there's John," Mama said suddenly as a figure loomed up ahead.

Elizabeth scrambled across the cracked vinyl seat and pressed her nose to the glass as Uncle John slid past the window, striding along.

"Shouldn't we stop?" she said.

Mama looked at Elizabeth and then at Grandpa. "It does look like rain," she murmured.

Grandpa didn't even slow down. "Boy wants to walk," he said curtly.

Elizabeth watched out the back as Uncle John grew tinier in the distance and then disappeared.

Mama stared straight ahead. "He's not a boy," she said.

It was starting to sprinkle as they pulled into Craigsville. They let Mama off at the grocery store, and Elizabeth climbed over into the front seat and sat cross-legged.

Grandpa grinned at her. "Whatta say we have some ice cream first?"

"Yes, yes, yes," said Elizabeth, bouncing up and down.

Sitting in Ruby's on a tall silver swivel stool with a red vinyl top, Elizabeth felt like a movie star. She and Grandpa both ordered chocolate. Grandpa finished his in about six bites, but Elizabeth savored hers, wanting the moment to last. Soon it was dripping down the sides of the cone, and she couldn't lick it off fast enough. It was all over her chin and running down her arms.

Grandpa was laughing. Elizabeth was glad Mama wasn't there.

She finally bit off the bottom of the cone, sucked the rest of the ice cream out, and finished up the cone. They used a lot of napkins and mopped up as best they could, but Elizabeth was still sticky.

Then they went to the hardware store, a low, flat building with a tin roof. There was no sign out front but everyone called it Charlie's.

Charlie was rolling wooden barrels of nails into the store and nodded at Grandpa.

Behind the counter was a big box with little whimpering sounds coming from it. Elizabeth left Grandpa and went to see what was in it. Six pairs of soft brown eyes looked up at her.

"Puppies!" she gasped, sinking to her knees. She reached out an arm, and immediately the pups were all over her, jumping and licking, fighting for the touch of her hand.

"They's beagles. Ya wanta hold one?" Charlie offered. Grandpa was standing beside him.

One puppy was sitting off to the side, not joining in with the mob fighting over her arm. When Elizabeth looked at it, the puppy wagged its tail.

"That one's a little girl," said Charlie, picking it up by the scruff of the neck and depositing it in Elizabeth's lap. The pup was white with big black and brown spots on her back and soft brown ears. Her head was the softest thing Elizabeth had ever touched—softer than a flower petal, as soft as . . .

"Velvet!" Elizabeth said. "Her name is Velvet!"

Grandpa and Charlie laughed and moved off. It began to rain, and the store filled with people coming in out of the wet. Elizabeth saw Uncle John come in, dusting drops off the shoulders of the old army coat he always wore. He had caught up with them while they ate ice cream. He didn't look her way but went to sit in a darkened corner. Grandpa paid no notice of him.

The rain beat down so heavily on the tin roof that Elizabeth, glancing up, couldn't hear a thing the men were saying, although their mouths were moving.

They were trapped by the rain and couldn't go get Mama. She would have to wait. Elizabeth smiled to herself and snuggled down in a corner on a burlap sack, leaning against a nail keg with Velvet in her arms.

The puppy began methodically licking the ice cream off Elizabeth's arms and then working on her chin.

It tickled, and Elizabeth giggled. She felt very happy and sort of sleepy. Velvet was sleepy too, and they both curled up on the sack.

The rain was stopping and she heard Mama's voice. ". . . thought it would never stop. I left the bags over at the store. Where's Elizabeth?"

Grandpa pointed and Mama looked at Elizabeth, dozing on the burlap sack with a puppy in her arms.

"Time to go home, Elizabeth," Grandpa said. "Put the little feller back."

Elizabeth hid her face in Velvet's fur. A longing rose up inside her chest.

"How much for the puppy?" Mama said.

Charlie laughed. "They's free. We're trying to get rid of 'em. Give ya the whole litter if ya want." He turned to Grandpa.

"I already got me a hound dog," Grandpa said.

Mama faced Grandpa and put her hands on her hips.

"Well, this dog is going to be a pet," she said crisply.

For a heartbeat, nobody moved. Elizabeth scrambled to her feet. "I'll keep her in my room," she said.

Everybody laughed. Dogs weren't allowed in the yard, let alone the house.

"No dog's gonna ride in that car," Grandpa made one last stand.

The store got quiet as people moved back outside. Elizabeth's heart sank.

Suddenly Uncle John appeared out of the shadows, brushed past his father, and walked up to Elizabeth. He was breathing hard. Silently, he took the pup from her, turned, and headed out the door toward home. Grandpa watched him go.

Mama put an arm around Elizabeth's shoulders. "What shall we name her?" she said. Her eyes were bright. Her lipstick was mostly off, and her hair was windblown and wet from the rain. Elizabeth thought she was beautiful.

"Her name is Velvet," she said carefully so she wouldn't cry from happiness.

# Chapter 11

## *Uncle John's Secret*

"THERE HE GOES again," Elizabeth remarked to Velvet, curled on her lap.

Every day about that time, she would see Uncle John start up the mountain carrying two zinc buckets. From the way he plodded, she knew there was something heavy in them.

Elizabeth had only been up to the high pastures once, to get fence rails with Grandpa, but she knew the family kept sheep up there in the summer months because it was good grazing. But what was Uncle John going up there for every day, and what was in the buckets?

No one else seemed to notice or care. It was almost as if Uncle John had an invisible cloak, like a prince in a fairy story. Elizabeth had determined this was the day she was going to find out what was going on. She hopped up, the puppy sliding from her lap, and stuffed her feet into her boots. There were rocks on the mountain and she couldn't be barefoot.

Of course he knew she was following him, she reminded herself. But still Elizabeth hid, hunkering down in the tall grasses of the field whenever she thought he was looking back. He crossed the creek on the footbridge, and Elizabeth shucked off her boots and waded across farther down.

The cold water rippled around her ankles, and little rocks on the bottom hurt her feet. A crayfish skittered under a rock. She looked up just in time to see Uncle John disappear into the edge of the woods at the foot of the mountain. Elizabeth hurried after him.

The road made by the wagon was overgrown, and trees and bushes reached in from all sides to pull at her dress. Elizabeth wished she had Snowball to ride, but then she wouldn't be able to hide behind each tree like an Indian.

The trail wound up the mountain, and Elizabeth lost sight of Uncle John from time to time. It didn't matter, though—she knew he was going to the high meadow. It was a long walk, and Elizabeth was panting and could feel her heart beating in her ears.

Suddenly Uncle John stepped out from behind a tree. Elizabeth stopped dead, breathing hard. Uncle John was breathing hard too.

"Whatta you want?" he said. His face looked scared.

"Nothin'," Elizabeth croaked.

For a minute there wasn't a sound. A hush seemed to fall over the forest. Elizabeth wondered if she had gone deaf. Then Uncle John turned and started back up the mountain, trudging a slow, steady step.

Elizabeth didn't know what to do. Was he angry? Should she go back? But he had spoken to her, so she began to follow hesitantly and then a little faster. Soon she was walking close behind him in his footsteps.

As they came over the rise into the high meadow, he stopped and put the buckets down and she walked up beside him and stopped too. It felt natural—like she would have done with Daddy or Grandpa. They both breathed in the sweet-smelling scent of the wildflowers and watched the grasses ripple in the breeze. Over in the shade and out of the midday sun, the sheep had curled themselves into fluffy white marshmallows in the grass.

Uncle John grabbed the handles of the buckets again and headed for the far side of the meadow. But the toe of his boot caught an exposed root, and he tripped—going down on one knee and putting down a hand to catch himself. He hung onto one bucket, setting it down hard, but the other one landed on its side with a clunk, spilling the contents.

Little plants tumbled to the ground and Elizabeth realized that both buckets were filled with tiny plants, each one's roots wrapped in a piece of dampened burlap sack.

Uncle John slowly got to his feet, eyes fixed on the half-empty bucket. Red crept up his neck and onto his face and ears. He kicked the bucket with such force that it sailed fifteen feet away, and then with a howl he turned toward the nearest tree, grabbed either side of the trunk, and began to hit his forehead against it.

Elizabeth stood with her mouth open for a split second. Then she ran to his side. "Oh, please don't," she begged in a frightened voice, tears in her eyes.

"Stupid . . . stupid!" he said and continued the pounding.

She put her hand on his arm. "Please stop," she said more evenly.

Uncle John stopped and looked at her. He dropped to his knees beside the spilled plants and clasped his hands around his head and rocked back and forth, making a moaning sound.

Quickly Elizabeth retrieved the bucket and gently put the plants back in—checking the other bucket to see how they'd been arranged. She rewrapped the few that had come out of the burlap and tucked them into the rest. Then she set both buckets before him and knelt on the ground. "It's all right," she said.

The rocking continued.

"Uncle John, it's OK."

He stopped rocking and raised his head a bit and looked at the buckets. Then he looked in her eyes.

She gave him a tentative smile.

He got to his feet, a purple bruise starting on his forehead, and reached for the buckets. Elizabeth put out her hand carefully and took one of them from him. He turned and started across the meadow again. Elizabeth took a deep breath and followed.

On the other side of the field, Uncle John had sectioned off a secret garden for himself, surrounded by rocks. It was not a large garden but was filled with the most exquisite flowers and plants Elizabeth had ever seen.

"Where did you get these?" she said in delight. But then she knew—the mail-order seed catalog she'd seen him reading, those brown paper packages he brought back from the post office in Calvin. Maybe he'd been growing seedlings in his room.

Uncle John went right to work with a hoe, digging a trench for the new plants they'd brought. Elizabeth hesitated just a moment and then took a plant out of the bucket, unrolled the burlap, and positioned it in the rich earth.

And Uncle John didn't say a word, didn't look up, just kept chunking at the soil. So Elizabeth took another plant, her heart light in her chest.

# Chapter 12

## *Family Reunion*

IT WAS THE day of the family reunion, and Grandma was up even earlier than usual, clanging around the kitchen. But Elizabeth just rolled over, gazed at the blue-flowered wallpaper and dozed off again.

A little later in the morning, Mama called up the steps. "Time to get up, girls. Reunion time!"

Annie was awake immediately and talking to her doll. "Now, Lulu, time to get ready for the reunion." She was lying on her back, head propped up on her goose-down pillow. She held Lulu above her and looked earnestly into her eyes. The doll's soft body drooped down.

Downstairs there was a flurry of activity. Grandma and Mama were carrying hot dishes wrapped in dish towels through the living room to the side door. Then Grandpa and Daddy, wearing fresh shirts and with their hair wetted down, took them down the porch steps and out the gate to the waiting flatbed wagon. Fannie and Maud stood patiently in their traces, swatting flies with their long tails.

Elizabeth swung on the big porch swing in her nightgown and sniffed the air. Smelled like fried chicken and cornbread and maybe a raspberry cobbler.

"Lizzie, you get upstairs and get dressed," Mama said impatiently. She was tired of cooking and would rather be reading her book, Elizabeth guessed. "Your clothes are on the bed."

Aunt Lorena was minding Sarah, who had a pink dress on over her diaper and a bonnet she was trying to pull off.

Elizabeth climbed upstairs to discover Mama had left out her blue Sunday-go-to-meetin' dress. She put it on grumpily, leaving her nightgown in a heap on the bed.

"Elizabeth, would you fill the water jug?" Grandma said.

Elizabeth banged out onto the back porch, poured water into the top of the pump, and began working the handle furiously. Water spurted out.

Turning back to the house, Elizabeth saw Uncle John sitting on the bench at the end of the porch by the outside door to his room. Whichone's box was under the bench.

Uncle John didn't look up. He was dressed just like always in a soft shirt, suspenders, black pants, and high leather boots that tied up the front. His dark hair wasn't combed.

He wasn't dressed for the reunion.

He wasn't going.

Lately the things Elizabeth wanted to say to Uncle John, wanted to ask him, were well-nigh unbearable— like bees trapped in a quart jar. She stepped up on the porch with the jug of water and hesitated, willing him to look up.

Whichone jumped out of her box, leaving squalling kittens behind, and got in his lap to be petted. He scratched along her back and she purred.

"Aren't you going?" Elizabeth burst out.

His eyes never left the cat's back, dark brows drawn together in concentration.

There was a moment of silence. Then Uncle John's bright blue eyes suddenly met hers. "Too many people."

Elizabeth swelled with joy when he spoke to her, like someone blew up a balloon in her chest.

"Elizabeth Rose, let's go," Mama called from inside.

Uncle John's eyes dropped, and he resumed petting the cat, only faster.

Elizabeth opened the screen door, fumbled with the latch, and carried the heavy jug inside.

"What are you doin' out there so long?"

"Nothin', Mama."

"Take that jug and this tin of cookies and put them in the wagon. Tell your Daddy I'll be right there."

*Family Reunion*

Elizabeth did as she was told. On the long, hot wagon ride to the church, nothing bothered her—not the yellow jackets gathering around the covered dishes, not Annie singing the two words *amazing grace* over and over. She sat on the back of the wagon with the tailgate down and swung her legs, letting the chicory and the tall grasses tickle her bare feet.

At the church, wagons and a few cars were pulled up on the grassy field out to the south of the cemetery. The white clapboard church sat on an acre of newly mown grass. Grandpa and his boys had helped build Alderson Baptist Church with lumber donated from their property. Family from all over the state gathered each summer for the annual family reunion.

Aunt Louella and Aunt Myrtle were in flowered dresses with big hats to protect them from the sun. Aunt Lorena, young and high-spirited, let her hair down to glisten in the sun. If anyone asked her where her hat was, she just laughed and said nobody wore hats in Charleston.

The men carried all the dishes to the tables made out of boards and sawhorses, set end to end across the lawn and spread with oilcloth. After much discussion, one table was laid with meats, another with vegetables, a third with breads and jams. Two tables were needed for all the pies and cakes. Blankets were spread on the grass for sitting and eating.

All of Elizabeth's twenty-five first cousins were there. The boys ran screeching down to the river near the church, where they shucked off their clothes and swam naked. The girls weren't allowed near. The older girls sat in the shade and told secrets, picked daisies and plucked them clean for "he loves me, he loves me not," and wove flowers into chains for their hair.

Elizabeth played Red Rover for a while with some of the younger girls. Cousin Patricia Sue was on the other side. "Red Rover, Red Rover, let Patsy come over!" Elizabeth chanted, holding hands with cousins Delores Ann, Mary Ann, and Betty Ruth.

Later she and Patsy played "Salt and Pepper" with Annie. "Do you want salt or pepper?" they asked her innocently. Patsy was holding Annie's upper body, her arms wrapped under Annie's arms and clasped across her chest. Elizabeth had hold of Annie's feet.

Annie considered. "Salt!" she shouted. She had played the game before.

Patsy and Elizabeth swung her back and forth and then shook her up and down gently.

"Now pepper!" Patsy yelled, and they shook her up and down really fast so that her curls bounced all over and she squealed.

"Dinner! Diiiinnner . . . " the women were calling.

Daddy went to fetch the boys.

It was while Elizabeth was standing in line that she got an idea. She slipped a second plate and put it under hers. She filled her plate, ran to sit under the tree in the shade while she ate, and then got back in line a second time.

Mama was shooing the flies off the pies. "Elizabeth Rose, didn't I see you go through here just now?" she put her hands on her hips.

"Mama, I'm just starved and everything's so good," Elizabeth said in her whiney voice.

"Mind you don't take the last of anything now." Mama was pleased. She liked for people to eat up.

"I won't, Mama."

First she chose two chicken breasts because she knew Uncle John liked white meat, then mashed potatoes, green beans, baked beans, whole green onions, applesauce, tomatoes, cornbread, and biscuits. On top of all this she made sure no one was looking and quickly piled on pieces of buttermilk pie and raspberry cobbler. She snatched a dish towel off the table, covered the plate, and started for their wagon.

"Where're you headin', girl?" Uncle Dan said, coughing. He was a coal miner—tall, rawboned, with a kindly face, coal dust permanently outlining the knuckles of his hands.

"Gonna eat at the wagon away from all those yellow jackets," she said pertly.

He snorted. "Afraid of a few bees! They won't eat much." But he let her pass.

No one was at the wagons, and the horses were all tied to a nearby shade tree, dozing in the heat, heads down, tails switching, back left hoof bent in a resting pose.

The tailgate was still down on their wagon. Elizabeth placed the plate carefully on the rough boards of the wagon bed and scrambled up. Then she lifted the heavy lid to the toolbox built into the side of the wagon. There among the tools, carried in case the wagon broke down, she carefully placed the plate.

It was dusk as they headed home. Elizabeth stretched out on the tool box and pretended to be asleep.

"That child is plum tuckered out," Grandma said.

"I'll unload the wagon, Mama," Elizabeth said eagerly when they got home. "You all just go on into the kitchen, and I'll bring everything in to be washed up."

The half empty pans and dishes she carried through the side of the house, through the living room, through the dining room, and into the kitchen. But Uncle John's plate she sneaked around the back of the house in the gathering dusk and set down with a muffled *clunk* right in front of the outside door to his room.

She watched from behind the rain barrel for a moment and then dashed back to finish the wagon.

Before bed she went out to check on the plate and it was gone. No sound from Uncle John's room, and she hadn't seen him all evening. Could a possum have gotten the food? A raccoon? Wouldn't they have left the dish?

She lay awake that night for a bit, watching the light from the potbellied stove downstairs flicker in the stairwell.

In the morning Elizabeth woke to the sound of drops splattering against the window panes. Mama was shaking her shoulder. "Elizabeth, wake up, honey. Grandma's arthritis is acting up this morning. Think you can feed the chickens and get the eggs by yourself?"

Elizabeth crawled out of bed and pulled on her dress and a sweater. Outside it was cold and damp, but the kitchen was warm and lit by an oil lamp. The fire in the cookstove was stoked up high, and Mama was rolling out biscuits on the counter in Grandma's stead and dishing up bowls of oatmeal. Grandpa was standing on the back porch, eating his and watching the rain. He was wearing a slicker because he had to go milk the cows.

Elizabeth took her bowl to the small kitchen table opposite Uncle John, who was piling on the brown sugar and didn't look up as usual. She wasn't used to being up this early and wanted to be back in bed. She nibbled the oatmeal off her spoon with her teeth and felt miserable. Why did everything on the farm have to be done so early in the morning?

After Daddy and Grandpa had gone to tend the livestock, she went into the darkened living room and rummaged around the old coat tree until she found an umbrella and then looked for her cowboy boots. They were sitting neatly over to the side, and she sat down on one of the highback chairs to put them on. A piece of paper was sticking out of one, and she pulled it out and smoothed it across her knee, leaning toward the window to capture the light.

It was a drawing of Snowball! It was done in a soft pencil and was mostly just his head with some of his sturdy neck showing. His mane was a mess like usual, falling in all directions and sticking straight up and getting in his eyes. You could see the blue eye on the white side of his face but the brown eye on the black side of his face just peeked out of his mane. Both ears were forward, and he had a mouthful of hay and looked all content. Elizabeth had seen him look that way a hundred times.

She couldn't stop looking at the picture. Before she put her boots on, she ran back up the stairs, taking them two at a time. Annie was a roll of blankets in the bed, and the rain was streaming down the window.

Where could she hide it? Elizabeth looked around the room. Someplace she could take it out and look at it often. She opened her drawer in the big oak bureau against the wall. Under her underwear and socks was the white Bible Grandma had given her when she was baptized. She opened it to Psalms, in the middle, and carefully placed the picture of Snowball among the pages and closed the leather cover.

Hurriedly she closed the drawer and ran back down the stairs. But not before she whispered a prayer into the soft darkness of the room.

"Thank you, Jesus, that me and Uncle John are friends."

# Chapter 13

## *Apple-Blossom Time*

IT WAS SATURDAY afternoon, and Mama was making pies for Sunday dinner the next day because Grandma was sick and couldn't work. She huddled on the daybed under several blankets although it was warm and everything was blooming. Doc Evans was coming later, and Elizabeth didn't want to miss his visit.

Neither did Annie. "Let's play doctor with the dolls," Annie said.

"We can't," Elizabeth said, "we've got Sarah." They both knew Sarah would chew on the dolls' heads and fuss and interrupt their play.

"She needs a nap," Annie said hopefully, glaring at Sarah who was toddling around the living room putting everything on the floor—couch cushion on the floor, Elizabeth's book *The Boxcar Children* on the floor. She grabbed hold of the cord to the lamp and tugged on it.

"No, no Sarey," Elizabeth grabbed her baby sister away. "She'll never nap now. It's morning," she said to Annie over her shoulder. "Let's take her for a walk and make her tired." She added with sudden inspiration, "*And* . . . after the doctor comes, we'll know *how* to play doctor."

Annie accepted this promise, although her little rosy bow mouth puckered in distress. They each held one of Sarah's hands and went out on the side porch and across the lawn. Elizabeth undid the latch to the side gate and let them out.

"Let's go up to the apple trees," Elizabeth said, and they began a slow progression up the side of the north mountain.

But suddenly Snowball, munching on a mouthful of daisies, tousled mane over his eyes, raised his head up in front of them. He was so short that when he put his head down to graze, he was almost hidden in the field flowers and grasses.

"You two can ride Snowball," Elizabeth said triumphantly. "Then we'll go faster."

"Yay!" said Annie, jumping up and down.

Sarah screeched in delight at Annie.

Elizabeth sidled up to Snowball and gently took hold of the halter he always wore. The halter was like a bridle without reins or a bit between his teeth. The pony followed her obediently to where her two sisters were waiting in the tall grass.

"Don't we need the saddle?" Annie said. "Don't we need the bridle?" Annie was always asking questions.

"You can ride him bareback, and I'll lead him by his halter," Elizabeth said.

First she got Annie on; that part was easy. She led Snowball to the fence and Annie climbed up, swung one leg over and was on.

Sarah stood barefoot in the field, her sturdy little legs planted, blue eyes wide, a wilting daisy in one pudgy hand. She was wearing only a cloth diaper and plastic pants.

Elizabeth picked her up clumsily and walked to the patient pony.

"Put her behind," Annie said. She always had to ride behind Elizabeth.

"No, let's put her in front so you can keep her from falling off," Elizabeth said. Finally Elizabeth had Sarah settled on Snowball's back in front of Annie.

"She smells like poopie," said Annie, taking advantage of no grown-ups around.

"Mama just changed her and you're not supposed to say that," Elizabeth said, and she started to lead the pony up the mountain. "Hold onto his mane and squeeze his back with your knees," she instructed Annie.

The mountains stood proud in the spring sunshine, smiling down on them. Elizabeth felt happy.

"Knock, knock," she said to Annie.

"Who's there?" Annie responded promptly.

"Who," Elizabeth said.

"Who *who?*" Annie said innocently.

Elizabeth laughed merrily. "*You* don't whooo—*owls* do!"

Annie shrieked with laughter, and Sarah looked back and forth between her two sisters, craning her neck to see Annie.

The grasses brushed Snowball's shoulders and tickled the girls' feet. Annie leaned down and plucked the head off a Queen Anne's Lace and showed it to Sarah. Then Sarah tried to lean over and get one.

"No, Sarey." Elizabeth pushed her back upright and then picked the flower and offered it to her. Sarah promptly stuck her little nose into the center.

"It don't smell good," Annie laughed at her. Then she whispered proudly in Sarah's ear, "Queen Anne's Lace is named for me."

Elizabeth knew that wasn't true, but she didn't say anything. Daddy had told her a particular white rose was named the Elizabeth Rose when she was younger. Daddy was always making up lovely stories.

Now the mountain got steeper, and Snowball labored to climb. Annie, one arm around Sarah's waist, leaned forward into her and Elizabeth kept a hand on the baby's arm. Then they were over the top and into the orchard, and there ahead of them were the apple trees, blossoms drifting softly down and covering the grass with a blanket of white.

Annie slipped to the ground and ran to the trees, and Elizabeth lifted Sarah down and set her on her feet. But Sarah sat down—*plump* on her diapered bottom—and began carefully picking up the white flowers from the grass.

Star-shaped blossoms rained down on the little group, landing in Snowball's black mane, nestling in Sarah's dark curls, and catching on Annie's eyelashes.

Elizabeth raised her hands to the soft petal shower in joy. "Annie!" she said. "It's snowing!"

Annie spun around and around until she got dizzy and fell down. Lying on her back staring up into the apple trees, she opened her mouth to catch the flowers.

"Don't *eat* them, silly," Elizabeth said, laughing.

"But we eat snowflakes." Annie propped herself on her elbows.

Now Sarah was trying it, picking up a blossom with dexterous little fingers and placing it on her tongue.

"No-no, Sarey," Elizabeth said. Then she got an idea. "I know! Let's pretend we're lost in a snowstorm!"

Annie sat up, eyes bright. "And *then* what happens, Lizzie?"

Elizabeth concentrated. "We went out to get firewood for our poor, sick grandma, but then a blizzard came and we couldn't find our way back home."

"Here's the firewood." Annie jumped up and began collecting sticks from under the drifting flowers, ankle deep around the girls.

"And we're freezing." Elizabeth folded her arms across her chest and began to shake and chatter her teeth.

Annie's eyes were big and liquid. "And we miss our mama, right Lizzie?"

"And we dream about home and our soft bed and warm fire." Elizabeth sat down in the grass beside Annie, scraping tiny flowers together with her hands until her sister was buried to her waist.

Sarah was still seated in her little pile of blossoms, trying to get the little flower off her tongue. She was too busy to be lost in a blizzard. Snowball had wandered off, grazing as he went.

"And then . . ." Elizabeth said, pausing dramatically.

"What?" Annie said with eyes and mouth round.

"Then a *wolf* comes!" Elizabeth made her voice menacing.

Annie shrieked in terror, startling Sarah, who began to cry.

"What's going on here?" It was Grandpa, tromping up over the rim of the mountain. "Been looking for you girls."

"Grandpa!" Annie ran to him and threw her arms around his soft black pants. She turned her little face up to him.

"We were hunting up firewood and got lost in the snow and then a *wolf* came," she said dramatically, imitating Elizabeth's tone of voice.

Grandpa looked at Elizabeth. "You scarin' these younguns?"

"We were just pretending the flowers were snow," Elizabeth said, embarrassed.

"Well, we better get you girls in out of the cold," Grandpa said with a twinkle in his eyes. He picked up Sarah and started back toward the farmhouse.

"Grandpa, Grandpa, don't forget the firewood!" Annie said in distress.

Grandpa didn't look back. "You girls bring it on. We'll put it in the cookstove tonight."

Elizabeth still felt cold from the pretend blizzard and rubbed her bare arms. Then she grabbed a handful of flowers and threw them—*splat*—at the back of Annie's curly head.

"Snowball fight!" she yelled. She was glad Grandpa was there to take charge and she could be a kid again.

She and Annie threw snowballs at each other until they reached the edge of the mountain. The old farmhouse was nestled in the trees below, and smoke came out of the chimney and drifted off into the blue distance. The doctor's pickup truck labored up the long dirt drive.

Elizabeth flew down the hill, braids swinging behind.

"I'm going to ride the running board," she yelled over her shoulder.

# Chapter 14

## *A Day with Grandma*

ELIZABETH HADN'T SEEN Uncle John for days. "Where's Uncle John?" she asked Grandma, trailing along behind her to check on the baby chicks just hatched the previous week. Grandpa had built three tiny houses, just chicken size, out on the side of the bank, and Grandma had put a hen in each house with a dozen eggs to sit on.

"Probably feeling poorly," Grandma said, scattering grain from the bulging apron that she had tucked up in front. Chickens, reddish-brown feathers glistening in the sun, squawked and fought over the food.

"What's the matter with him?" Elizabeth took a handful from the apron and sprinkled it on the chickens' backs. She liked to watch them peck corn off each other.

"Lord only knows, chile."

"Maybe he's just sad," Elizabeth said.

Grandma stopped and looked at her. Then with effort she got down on her knees in front of one of the little houses and, reaching inside, brought out a fluffy black chick. She presented it to Elizabeth.

"Peep, peep, peep!" said the chick.

"Peep, peep, peep!" said his brothers and sisters from inside the little house.

"He's so cute!" Elizabeth cooed over the ball of down, cupping it in her hands and kissing it on the top of its head. The chick watched her with little beady black eyes that glittered like the onyx beads in Grandma's Sunday-go-to-meetin' necklace.

The mother hen was pecking at a piece of crushed eggshell, paying no attention to Elizabeth and the chick.

Gently Elizabeth stroked the sharp beak and tried to get the chick to grasp her finger with its clawlike toes.

"Can I bring him back to the house? Please, Grandma." She knew Grandma would let her.

"Just for a bit. He needs to be with his mama." Grandma took off the floppy straw hat that she wore in the sun and fanned herself. "Who-eee, it's hot." She wiped back a strand of damp hair. Grandma's gray hair had never been cut. Every day she wore it braided and wound around in a bun fastened at the back of her neck with hairpins.

They whisked the chick off and headed toward the farmhouse.

"Do you think she'll know it's gone?" Elizabeth asked.

"No, not likely," Grandma smiled, dusting the whitish chaff from the grain off her hands.

"Maybe she'll count them." Elizabeth teased, looking back over her shoulder dramatically. They both laughed.

"Well, maybe she will, and she'll come looking for us, and we'll have to give him back."

"What will I name him?" Every animal, no matter how small, had to have a name.

"How about Blackie?" Grandma suggested. "He's the only black one."

"Blackie." Elizabeth held the chick up at eye height and said the name aloud to see its reaction. "I name you Blackie," she pronounced, kissing it on the head again.

"You're gonna kiss the fuzz right off his head and he'll be bald like Great Uncle Wilson," Grandma said. They both laughed.

Grandma was lighthearted. She had been sick, but she seemed to be feeling better. Grandpa was at the Millers' farm helping out. Daddy had driven Mama to Dr. Lawson's office for Sarah's checkup, and Annie had gone along. No one knew where Uncle John was.

Everyone was gone but Elizabeth so Grandma didn't have to fix a big dinner in the middle of the day.

They came in the side gate, across the porch, and into the upper room. Inside the farmhouse it was cooler, and they were grateful for that. Grandma disappeared into her bedroom.

Elizabeth continued into the living room and saw Velvet napping on the cool linoleum under the dining room table. She stopped to stroke her silky side and the puppy's tail went *bap, bap, bap* against the floor in greeting.

Elizabeth climbed up on the daybed and put Blackie carefully in the center of one of the pillows. She stroked his fuzzy side. Tiny gray lids covered his little eyes and he slept. Carefully, Elizabeth rolled over on her back and looked around the room at all the familiar objects.

On the wall over the bed was a framed cross-stitch saying Aunt Luella had made for Grandma and Grandpa's fiftieth anniversary.

> *Hours Fly*
> *Flowers Die*
> *New Days*
> *New Ways*
> *Pass By*
> *Love Stays*

At the end of the bed stood a massive wooden dresser of cherry wood. On the top under Grandma's Bible was a lacey white doily. A little stub of a pencil attached to a string hung from between the pages. Grandma made a small mark at the top of each chapter after she read it. Each chapter had a lot of marks.

Beside the Bible squatted the plastic radio Daddy had brought with them from New Mexico. Elizabeth always hoped to hear *Mockingbird Hill* again. She sang it softly now as a lullaby for Blackie.

*Tra la la*
*Tweedle dee dee dee*
*It gives me a thrill*
*To wake up in the morning*
*To the mockingbird's trill*

*Tra la la*
*Tweedle dee dee dee*
*There's peace and good will*
*You're welcome as the flowers*
*On Mockingbird Hill*

"Land sakes, it's *so* hot." Grandma sat down with a *plop* in the big rocker in the corner of the upper room. "Could you run fetch Grandma's fan?" she called in to Elizabeth.

Grandma's fans were beside the daybed in the living room. Elizabeth got the everyday fan, not the Sunday church one. The everyday one had roses painted on it and folded up tight. The Sunday fan was from Japan; Uncle Joe had brought it back for Grandma after the war. It didn't fold but was on a stick and had a beautiful scene of a lady in a long dress under a funny tree. She stepped up into the upper room.

Grandma took the fan thankfully, snapped it open, and fluttered it back and forth. Every now and then she would turn her hand and fan Elizabeth for a while. Then she opened up her sewing basket, got out a pair of scissors, and began to cut old dresses into squares. She didn't measure them but each square came out the exact same size.

Elizabeth dug in the sewing basket and stuck a silver thimble on her finger.

"Guess what *I'm* doing," Grandma said.

"Making a quilt." Elizabeth was digging for the pin cushion. It was red and fat and had straight pins embedded in it, only their shiny heads showing.

"Not just *any* old quilt. This one's for my namesake."

It took Elizabeth a minute to get it. "For me?!"

"Going to make you a round-the-world quilt like the one in your Aunt Lorena's room."

Elizabeth loved Aunt Lorena's room. Grandpa had made her a *real* dressing table with a mirror when she turned sixteen. It even had a white skirt, attached with thumbtacks, that Grandma had made out of flour-sack cloth. On top there was a cut glass dish holding a powder puff. The room had a double bed, covered with the round-the-world quilt. It started in the center with one square and the others spiraled out and swirled around it like the ripples from a stone thrown in a pond.

"You get to pick the piece for the center," Grandma said importantly. Her eyes sparkled behind her glasses. She dumped a paper grocery bag full of squares between them.

Elizabeth dipped her arms up to the elbows in the beautiful pieces of cloth. Grandma's gnarled hands with their paper-thin skin trembled as she reached for a piece of white satin.

"This be leftover cloth from my wedding dress," she said, "when I married your grandpa almost sixty-two years ago."

Elizabeth stroked it against her cheek. Then she spotted a soft red piece of cloth. "What's this from, Grandma?"

Grandma hesitated. "That's from a shirt your uncle John wore to that dance. He had me make it special."

"Uncle John went to a dance!"

"Yessiree! Your uncle John could really dance and play the fiddle. But *that* night . . ." Grandma trailed off, gazing out the window at the hills in the distance.

"What, Grandma? What happened that night?" Elizabeth got up on her knees.

Grandma took a long time threading her needle, biting on the end of the thread to make it into a point and tying a knot at the other end with arthritic fingers. She peered over her glasses at Elizabeth.

"Tell me!" Elizabeth pulled the sleeve of Grandma's dress. "Pretty please with sugar on it," she added with feeling.

"Pearly was going to be there, and he was sweet on her." The words poured out of Grandma's mouth like she'd been holding them back a long time. "But she showed up with a new beau and John had done gone and dressed all up. It was snowing, and he ran out without his coat and walked the four miles home. When we got back, he was in bed with the chills and got pneumonia. Nearly died."

Grandma's old eyes were moist, her voice low. "We put him in the hospital at Summersville for six weeks. Your grandpa had to sell Buttercup to pay for it."

Elizabeth's heart hurt in her chest.

"John was always different," Grandma said, distantly, "but after that he got worse—sorta withdrew. Doctor said maybe it was the high fever." Grandma's mouth drew into a tight line, like she'd said too much. She began busily sorting through the scraps.

"I want the red piece for the center," Elizabeth said.

Grandma looked at her and then picked up the old shirt and began to cut.

"I'll get you a drink of water, Grandma." Elizabeth slipped down and went back into the living room. But instead of continuing into the kitchen, she went to the door of Uncle John's room and knocked softly.

No answer.

She knocked again.

No answer.

No one was allowed in Uncle John's room. Elizabeth's heart hammered but she opened the door and peeked in.

It was small, not much larger than the bed. There was a chair in the corner, and his fiddle stood on it. Books were in stacks against the walls. A door led out onto the back porch.

Then she looked at the walls, and her mouth opened in astonishment. Drawings were everywhere: the hayfield waving in the wind, the sun setting behind the barn, the apple trees in blossom on top of the mountain, Grandma stringing beans in her chair by the fire with wisps of hair escaping from her bun.

There were sketches of Elizabeth and Annie and Sarah holding kittens, Grandpa with Patrick the Mule, Mama sitting cross-legged on the stool in the yard stirring apple butter in a big kettle, and Daddy tending his bees. And always the mountains—blue and overlapping into the distance.

Elizabeth closed the door quietly. She went back to Grandma carrying the chick.

Grandma looked at her carefully. "Where's my water, Little Miss Slowpoke?"

"I think I should take Blackie back to his mama," Elizabeth said.

"Good idea! Then we'll have us peanut butter sandwiches on store-boughten bread," Grandma said cheerfully. She held up the start of the quilt to show Elizabeth. The red square glowed in the center of several others.

"It's beautiful," Elizabeth sighed and ran to kiss Grandma's soft, crinkly cheek.

# Chapter 15

## *The Visiting Committee*

G RANDMA WAS VERY sick, Mama said, and they were to be quiet. Her mouth had that turned-down, worried look it used to have in New Mexico when she paid the bills.

Annie and Sarah didn't understand because they were little, Mama said, but Elizabeth did.

"Is Grandma going to die?" Elizabeth asked.

"No, of course not," Mama said, but her mouth got more worried.

The visiting committee from church came in an old school bus that had been painted blue with *Alderson Baptist Church* in white on the side. Elizabeth was sitting on the wide, flat banister to the front porch where in the winter Grandma swept off the snow and crumbled biscuits for the sparrows. She watched the bus coming around the side of the mountain, jouncing up the bumpy dirt track that led up to Grandma's house from the hard road.

Jed Phillips, the bus driver, pulled around in a circle down below the house and headed the front of the bus back the way he'd come. The Baptist youth group members, clustered in the back of the bus, peered out the small exit window at Elizabeth and the farmhouse.

Daddy came out on the front porch and stood with his hands on his hips. He wasn't wearing his hat, and his hair was freshly combed. The kitchen window up over the porch was open, and Elizabeth could hear clinking as Mama made coffee.

"Daddy," Elizabeth said with an ache in her chest, "is Grandma going to die?"

Daddy stared off into the mountains. He didn't say anything for a minute and then, "I hope not, Lizzie girl."

"Will she go to heaven if she dies?"

"If your grandma doesn't go to heaven, Lizzie, nobody's going."

Now people were getting off the bus and straggling up the hill in twos and threes. Several women from Christian Friendliness got off first, their heels sinking in the soft ground. They wore flowered dresses and flat hats that looked like pot lids. Stiff little veils matched each hat and stuck out over their foreheads.

Next came several of the church elders—hats in hand, faces red from fresh shaving. Jed turned off the ignition and walked up the hill with them, lighting a cigarette and puffing it quickly.

Rev. Brown came out next and paused. He was wearing the same black suit he wore winter and summer, but his bushy gray beard was newly trimmed. His head was partly bald, but the long white hair that was left scraggled over his collar. Rev. Brown looked around and sniffed the air. He opened the front gate to the yard to let the church ladies in and nodded up at the porch.

"Willie, Elizabeth Rose. A sad occasion."

Now the teens were getting off the bus. Cousin Clark was there, jostling with another boy and looking strange without his suspenders. The teenage girls were uncomfortable in stockings and walked like ducks in their white dress-up flats. They trooped up the sagging wooden steps to the front porch, and Elmer Fitzsimmons, who ran the newspaper, held the screen door. The men waited respectfully for all the ladies to go in.

Elizabeth trailed in after them into the crowded living room. Grandma was propped up on the daybed. Mama had helped her wash up a bit, and she was wearing a silky blue bed jacket that Aunt Lorena had brought from Charleston. Grandpa, looking stern, was sitting beside her bed on a high-backed chair.

Mama had pulled out all the dining room chairs so people would have a place to sit. Aunts and uncles and cousins were standing against the walls.

One of the ladies was holding Sarah and fussing over her. Annie was dancing a little jig on the linoleum like she'd seen Grandpa dance in the flatbed wagon to keep warm on cold days. Mama told her to stop, but Jed began stomping his foot and clapping his hands. "Ain't you something!" he said, laughing down at Annie.

Suddenly Annie got shy and crawled under the dining room table and peeked out from under the oilskin tablecloth.

All the women came over and held Grandma's hands and whispered earnestly into her face. Tears ran down Grandma's cheeks.

Rev. Brown cleared his throat to signal the start of the service, and the ladies all sat down, sniffing and wiping their noses with handkerchiefs, their veils quivering.

"Well now, Sister Rose," he began, raising his voice. "Life's a long, hard journey, and if we didn't have Jesus waiting there for us at the end of the road, what an awful thing that would be."

"Amen," Elmer said.

"But he *is* waiting there with his arms open wide to take us through the pearly gates to heaven." Reverend Brown raised his arms in a *V* and looked up through the ceiling.

"Praise the Lord," one of the women said.

Elizabeth slipped under the table with Annie, who started to protest, but Elizabeth shushed her and for once Annie minded. Velvet was hiding there too and

Elizabeth gathered the pup into her arms and stroked her soft ears. Annie had Lulu with her and had spread her blanket out to make a nest. She lay down on her blanket with her thumb in her mouth and looked like she might sleep.

Elizabeth tried to figure out who people were by their shoes. Suddenly, her glance fell on the bottom of Uncle John's bedroom door, back in the corner behind the dining room table, and she noticed that it was open just a crack. She forgot to breathe. Uncle John was watching.

Virgil, Grandma's cousin once removed, played the harmonica, and everyone sang "The Old Rugged Cross." Grandma had one of Grandpa's bandana handkerchiefs clutched in her hand.

"Now let us pray," Rev. Brown said. "Our Father, Who art in heaven . . ." he started into the Lord's Prayer.

Elizabeth knew you were supposed to keep your eyes closed when there was praying, but she couldn't help peeking at Uncle John's door.

"Amen," said Rev. Brown, and *amens* echoed around the room.

"Do you have any last wishes, Sister Rose?" Molly Hawkins said.

"There is one thing," Grandma said. She was dry-eyed. Her cheeks were flushed pink and suddenly she looked like a young girl.

Grandpa looked at her and everyone fell quiet.

"I want to hear my boy John play the fiddle," she said.

The door Elizabeth had been watching shut quickly and noiselessly.

Everybody knew John. They knew his brooding presence, his dark moods, his fits. They all knew the story of him and Pearly. Everybody was afraid of him.

Everybody but Elizabeth. She scrambled out from under the table, bumping her head softly on the edge. "I'll get him, Grandma."

All eyes turned on her. Mama was smiling at her with tears in her eyes.

Elizabeth went to John's door and knocked.

No answer.

Everyone watched in silence.

Elizabeth prayed to Jesus inside her head that Uncle John would grant Grandma's wish. She opened the door and went in.

Uncle John was sitting on the small wooden chair in the corner with his fiddle across his knees. He didn't look surprised to see her.

"You gotta come play."

"I cain't. Not with all them people."

"She's gonna die," Elizabeth said, feeling an empty black hole open up inside her.

There was a moment of silence. Then Uncle John stood up and followed Elizabeth out of the room.

Elizabeth snagged Whichone and climbed up on the daybed and lay down carefully beside Grandma.

Grandma put one arm around Elizabeth and stroked Whichone with the other hand. She never took her eyes off Uncle John.

Uncle John went to the center of the room where Annie had been dancing, put his fiddle under his chin, and drew the bow several times, turning the little screws.

Outside the window, the mountains leaned in, listening for the first note. Then the music soared—sweet and painful at the same time. Elizabeth closed her eyes and saw the high notes reaching up to heaven itself. She could see what heaven would be like for Grandma. Jesus would be there in his white robes, and there would be mountains, and it would be springtime when all the baby animals were born.

And Grandma wouldn't hurt anymore. And for that reason, Elizabeth could let her go.

And anyway . . . Elizabeth and Uncle John would always have each other.

*Contact Information*

To order additional copies of this book,
please visit
www.redemption-press.com.
Also available on Amazon.com and
BarnesandNoble.com.
Or by calling toll free 1 (888) 305-2967.